Fulltiming
for
New and Used
RVers

Cover design by Nick Inglish

Fulltiming for New and Used RVers, 2nd Edition
© 2011 RV Stuff

ISBN 978-1-56870-610-8

Second Edition

Printed in the United States of America
For information, contact:

RV Stuff
1116 Sea Pines Dr.
Savannah, Texas 76227
fulltiming@aboutrving.com

Table of Contents

About this Book

About this Author

Thinking About Fulltiming

What Else Do We Need To Know

Enough is Enough

About this Book

This book is about how to "think" about fulltiming—how you approach the idea, research the information, estimate your costs, look at what you need and don't need, and how you accomplish those normal daily things even though you will be (mostly) mobile—i.e., with no fixed physical location. Then, when you are ready to take the big step and actually fulltime, the book will provide lots of information to help you prevent mistakes during the transition and after you begin. This book will help you get ready to go and then actually go.

Fulltiming is definitely a change in lifestyle but not a negative change—not at all. A number of things in your life will change—we think for the better. It works for us.

But first, this book is…

- Not about trying to talk you into fulltiming. I would never attempt to talk you into this. You have to either want to or at least be intrigued enough by the idea that you are willing to try it.

- Not about "why" you should fulltime but "how" to fulltime.

- Not about gadgets or selling items ranging from RV lots to memberships to gadgets.

- Not about telling you to sell your house, get rid of your stuff, and just go.

My purpose here is to help make your decision easier when supported by solid information and by you making a "smarter" decision with facts and knowledge in hand.

The content is, to the best of my ability, factual, accurate, and current. While some suggestions are personal experience, they are verified by other fulltimers—sort of a consensus. Other suggestions were gleaned from research, manufacturer's recommendations, OEM's (Original Equipment Manufacturer) suggestions, and friends—with first-hand experience. However, all errors are mine.

At our seminars nationwide, many "newbies" and "wannabies" told us they were intrigued by the idea but finding good quality current information about how to get ready and then actually fulltime was difficult at best and often impossible. Sure, bits and pieces of information were scattered over the web, numerous magazine articles, various seminars, and always from well-intentioned friends (with or without experience).

I hope this collection of information helps.

Let me know if it does.

R. E. Jones
fulltime@aboutrving.com

About this Author

Ron Jones has been camping on wheels since 1962 when he purchased a small tent-trailer and immediately spent two weeks in the Great Smoky Mountains National Park. Through the years, he has owned pick-up campers, Class C, Class B (homemade), and Class A coaches. Plus, Ron has camped in tents, tent trailers, pick-up campers, and travel trailers—everything but a 5th wheel. He and Sandy (spouse) are fulltimers and meander just about anywhere in their diesel pusher across the USA and Canada.

Ron has retired (several times). He is retired Army (medical, 1970), retired Senior Professor of Engineering Technology at the University of North Texas (1998), and retired publisher (RonJon Publishing, Inc.) in 2006. Ron's hobbies are traveling, cooking, photography, writing, and eating out.

Ron writes (a lot). He was a columnist for Coast to Coast RV magazine, has written features for Motorhome, Highways, Family Motor Coaching, and Escapees magazines, is a contributor to the Good Sam Website (Weekly RV Tips), and has written a monthly article for CyberSam (the Good Sam digital newsletter). He has written ten books including numerous textbooks for public schools and colleges, how-to books, co-authored the best-selling RV book entitled *"All the Stuff You Need to Know About RVing"* (ISBN 1-56870-514-X), was a collaborator with Sandy on *"Wrinkle-Free RV Laundry"* (ISBN 978-156870-590-3), and released his new book, *"RVing to Alaska"* (ISBN 978-0-9825682-0-0) in January 2010.

Ron and Sandy present a variety of RV educational seminars nationwide at rallies, shows, and various gatherings. From driving topics to Hand Signals to how to pack your cooking liquids to the now famous "Sewage 101," their seminars are filled with great information, use professional-quality media, are laced with humor, and based on the idea that *"You don't know what you don't know."*

My Website

I launched my new website in July 2010 and there is nothing like it in the RV world. There are well over 100 RV-related articles available for your information. They are free, the information has been verified, and is credible. You can trust it.

There is a bit of overlap with my books but think of it this way... The details are in the books and the newer information is on my website—using both, you get it all.

Additionally, I included a lengthy list of "Unique Places" where you can visit unusual places and go to some of my first-class and no-class places to eat. Enjoy. Go to...

aboutrving.com

Thinking About Fulltiming

Fulltiming by Accident

Sandy and I have been fulltiming going on nine years now and the biggest surprise for most people is that we did not plan to fulltime—not at all. We both retired and our actual "plan" was to sell our lovely home in Denton, Texas that we had owned for sixteen years and move into something smaller. After all, we joked that we had bedrooms and bathrooms no one used or even walked into except to clean!

She and I agreed to focus on a condo—something where we would not have to deal with time-consuming constantly-recurring maintenance, yard work, and other common "house" stuff that keeps you busy. We simply wanted to get rid of the minutia, schedule, and structure that constantly ties you down as a result of home ownership. This was not a financial decision (we didn't have to sell) but more of a change-in-lifestyle decision—we just wanted to do something different other than take care of a house and yard.

Plus, during this same time, we had purchased a motorhome and really wanted to do some extensive travel. Since we were retired, all this was possible, and we planned to use the new condo as a "home base"—a place we could come back to. What a great plan! So, we put the house on the market.

Our house sold and the buyers wanted possession in three weeks—non-negotiable. So, we agreed and temporarily moved into our motorhome, packed and stored the sentimental "family" stuff while shedding an occasional tear, and turned our daughter and three grown grandkids loose on the other possessions (take anything you want from canned goods in the pantry to furniture to tools in the garage to the pictures on the wall). They did. We had one giant estate/yard/garage/junk sale with whatever was left (there was plenty left), made multiple trips to Goodwill, and the dumpster. We turned over the house to the new owners on time.

It was a three-week whirlwind packing, sale, and move so we decided to reward ourselves with a cross-country trip before we started looking for that condo—after all, our plan included lots of travel. So, off we went in our motorhome.

Eight years and two motorhomes later, we are still on that first trip! It worked for us. We still haven't looked at a condo! We still haven't looked back. We love this lifestyle!

We present RV seminars nationwide and are constantly asked when we will stop fulltiming. My consistent reply is that my last drive will be to the nursing home door where I will hand over the keys and they can help me inside.

Who Are Fulltimers

It just so happens that we are rarely inside a real house. With our particular RV lifestyle, actually going inside a house may happen only two or three times in the roughly eleven months we are traveling. We spend that twelfth month—Thanksgiving through Christmas—near our daughter and grandkids back in the Dallas area. They all have houses. I'm glad I don't.

During our eleven travel-months, when we happen to go into a house, I am constantly amazed. I find myself thinking, "What do they do with all this room?" I cannot imagine needing or even wanting all that excess space. Why would you want to have to take 20-25 steps to get from the kitchen to the bedroom?

Fulltiming is a radical change in lifestyle from typical day-to-day living in a house, apartment, or condo. [Author Note: I'm just going to use the word "house" and if something applies specifically to an apartment or condo, I will clarify it.] One common assumption is that someone who is a fulltimer has obviously considered this for a long time, perhaps even practiced it by RVing for a few years, possibly taken longer and longer trips, and owned or maybe rented several types or sizes of RVs to find the best one for them. Not so. Not even close! Sandy and I didn't have a single conversation about fulltiming before we started!

My changed perception started with close friends. They watched our new lifestyle (they were still working after we started fulltiming) and they decided to retire, sell their house, buy a motorhome, and fulltime. But neither one had ever spent a single night in an RV! Sure, they asked us thousands of questions to get started but they continue to fulltime today—about six years later. Their experience was the basis for one of my other books, *"All the Stuff You Need to Know About RVing."* Then, another set of friends decided to do the same thing—no experience there either—just a "dive in and do it" attitude. Both friends are still fulltiming today!

So fulltimers are made up of all kinds of RVers—young, old, experienced, no experience, working, and retired—what I call "New and Used RVers."

People fulltime for vastly different reasons. We have talked with young parents fulltiming and home-schooling their children so they could travel, visit, learn, and have their children experience this great nation firsthand. We met a retired couple from Tennessee whose three grown children lived in Colorado, Texas, and Maryland and fulltiming just made sense because they spent about a month visiting with each one before they move on to the next. Another couple told us that, because of their business, they never had the chance to travel. Plus, there have been several single seniors—both men and women—who said they were just tired of sitting around. The stories, reasons, and individuals that adopt the fulltiming lifestyle are endless.

> *A Personal Story... I've had lots of experience with RVs. I've been RVing (on wheels of some kind) since 1962 when I bought my first pop-up tent-trailer. I have nearly lost count but believe my current motorhome is my fifteenth RV of some type. Back in the 1980s, I bought a Champion (Class A) RV for $1.00 (that's one dollar!) from a guy that didn't want to license it. We used it locally for one season. Hey, you do what you can.*

Probably the most important characteristic for fulltiming with another person is that you get along—really well. Living in an RV, it is difficult to not be physically close to the other person virtually all the time. The joke is that if you burp, someone is always close enough to hear it.

Moving from a house into an RV—even a large RV—requires some change in daily behavior for everyone involved. For example, you just cannot create piles of stuff in the RV—there isn't that much floor space and the counter's surface area is extremely limited. Dirty laundry has to be put away someplace or you will trip over it —there simply isn't room to drop it on the floor and walk around it because there isn't room to walk around it. You will have less of everything with you—clothing, food, tools, etc. That's good.

Doing this, i.e., living in this fashion, is not hard and you don't have to deprive yourself of anything. We live very well— equal to or better than we did in our house. We do this with a lesser volume of stuff than before—in our house.

Why Would I Want To Fulltime

The information in this book will help any type of future fulltimer plan and prepare for their journey. "Fulltime" is a term applied to RVers who live and travel fulltime in their RVs. It does not mean "forever" nor does it imply that the RVers have gotten rid of everything (house, things) to be able to travel.

Lots of fulltimers are just on an extended trip—i.e., they may fulltime for several months or even a few years—and then return to their house. The classic "snowbird" (RVers who spend winters in warm climates and summers back in the north) is a perfect example of the extended traveler. They live and travel fulltime for some period of time—usually several months—but then typically return to their permanent "houses" to live there during warmer weather.

One "concern" often expressed by people thinking about fulltiming is what can they do to keep busy. Fulltimers typically need something to do. Assuming you retire, you really cannot just sit down and stay there very long—at minimum, it gets boring. Some fulltimers work, some volunteer, others find those parks where constant activities seem to be scheduled, some just bask in the sunshine, some fish, write, or play on the Internet, while others just want to travel. Simply, while fulltiming, you can manage to stay about as busy as you were when living in a house. The activities may be a bit different but you can certainly stay busy.

For example, there is a process called "work camping" (also called workamping and work kamping) and for our purposes, this is a situation where RVers trade labor for a campsite (and maybe some money). National and state parks, plus private campgrounds commonly offer seasonal work-camping opportunities such as maintenance, running an office or store, or camp host.

The thing you will lose by fulltiming is lots of "structure." Living in a house fixes you in one location (geographical area) where you work, visit, shop, eat, entertain yourself, and conduct most of your daily activities. If you are still working (not retired), then almost always, you are in an extremely structured environment—you get up at a certain time, go to work, function at your work, and return home at least five days per week. Even your weekends are structured with chores ranging from yard work to getting the car serviced to hair cuts.

Chores cause you to implement structure in your life—the more chores, the more structure. The RVing lifestyle naturally reduces the overall number of chores you have to do and yet, makes others more of a challenge to accomplish. For example, when RVing, there is no more yard work, painting a bedroom, cleaning the gutters, etc. However, you must continue to get an occasional haircut (well, many of us do). The challenge to RVers is where do you find a barber or hair salon while passing through Cut and Shoot, Texas or Sopchoppy, Florida?

When you begin fulltiming, the lack of structure provides a freedom typically unknown to homeowners and certainly never experienced by most people. RVers are not simply lost, meandering around, looking for something to do, or a place to settle down. Many will discover they fall in love with the freedom of the unstructured lifestyle—possibly for the first time in their lives and the RV lifestyle provides that potential for them. It's a grand feeling and the freedom is wonderful.

Is there any structure? Sure. You will need to pay bills, watch that certain TV show, take part in various activities, or schedule time with friends and family. For example, if you need to return to your home base for that special someone's birthday, graduation, or retirement party, then plan to be there. It is a structured event. However, when you start that part of your journey, the route you take, the sights you see, and other neat experiences you have on the way are totally yours to savor. We once were returning to the Dallas/Ft. Worth area (our home base) and it took us eight days to get there from Pecos, Texas (just 396 miles). Among other great places to visit, we stumbled onto the "West of the Pecos Museum" where Judge Roy Bean held court.

During our seminars, I tell people that "fulltiming is never a permanent decision." While that seems an unusual statement, think about fulltiming this way… at some future point in time, you will have to go off the road, that is, stop fulltiming. It could be that you might die—unfortunate, but a possibility. Most likely it would be for health reasons—your health may deteriorate or you might be in some accident. Another common reason is that family members (especially elderly parents) may require your help and you physically need to be close by. The point here is that while fulltiming is a major decision, it is not a permanent, locked-in-forever decision. You will always stop at some point.

When/if you do make the decision to fulltime, your non-RV friends will, for the most part, think you are a little crazy, but will be a bit envious of your new lifestyle—it's likely your family will, too. But don't listen to any of them.

Your family and friends will always be thinking that you are living out of some vehicle while you will be thinking that you are living in your home. After all, you sit in your favorite chair, know what is in every drawer, sleep in your own bed, know how and when the bed linens were laundered, and know what is in the fridge. Is that different from your house-bound friends—of course not. What is different is that you have the wonderful opportunity to wake up to whatever scenery you want out your front window—mountains, the beach, a desert, and whatever temperature or climate you want (within reason). For example, we don't do snow, period, and have managed to also avoid those Texas summers. So, you will hear this again: *You are at home (in your RV) but your RV is not (at home).*

The "Leap"—No RV Experience to Fulltime

My friends I mentioned earlier took the "leap" from living in a house to fulltiming in an RV—with no experience. Doing this has the potential for more error—i.e., bad decisions—and therefore more cost by having to pay for those bad decisions. The typical tendency is for new RVers to start out with a smaller unit in order to save cost. The logic goes something like this…

- The smaller RV will cost less
- It will be easier to resell if we don't like the lifestyle
- It will cost us less to operate.

It's flawed logic. Yes, they save some money on the purchase of the unit but often find that if they like the lifestyle, they most often trade for a larger unit—it's not uncommon for this to take place within the first year. Interestingly, most people like the lifestyle but want a bigger unit. Plus, they have no idea of the operational costs (due to no experience).

Taking the "leap" is expensive and exciting and will uproot your existing lifestyle in a positive way. While I do not have any data to verify this, I truly believe that of those who try it, the overwhelming majority stay with it.

If you are thinking of taking the "leap," know that many others have done this, too. I recommend a year for research—like the last year before you retire. This book will help plus guide you to other information resources that will prove invaluable in your research.

One unusual method for doing research is to visit a variety of dealers, several different RV shows, and rallies—especially the "Come-Home" type rally sponsored by various RV manufacturers. I recommend visiting two or three very large dealers and huge RV shows. Additionally, I often recommend visiting 10-15 different dealers! This will take time and effort to accomplish but this is a major financial decision as well as a lifestyle decision.

Doing this may require you to travel to other states but you may be able to save enough on the "deal" to offset your travel costs. However, the real reason is that you will simply see more options, floor plans, brands, deals, goodies, gadgets, accessories, and stuff. I absolutely believe that visiting a variety of dealers and shows will make you more knowledgeable and help you make a better purchasing decision. After all, you are going to spend $50,000 or $150,000 or $350,000 so investing into some serious research and time is likely to pay off in the long run.

Help Me With this Decision

You need lots of information to help make the decision to fulltime or for that extended trip. Our "no-experience" friends traded lots of e-mails with us and when we visited, had long talks to help them gain information. If you have friends that fulltime, they can be a great source of information. This will be a major change in lifestyle and planning will help you avoid mistakes— some of them costly. Therefore, the time and effort involved before taking the "leap" is worthwhile.

Fulltiming is a major decision so I do not recommend seriously considering information from anyone who is not currently fulltiming, i.e., their speculation or assumptions. This includes dealers, sales reps, or your brother/sister/mother/friend. While they may speculate with the best of intentions, you need to verify your information from experienced sources.

Information Sources

I have nothing against the local dealer in your town. But because of the large financial decision involved (especially if you are going to purchase a big motorhome) and the personal decision (especially if you are going to fulltime), you need some help. So I always recommend expanding your research—even if that local dealer is your brother!

Finding an RV is a very different process than finding a car. You can go to any medium-sized car dealer and see most or all their current models. Not so with RVs. There are only a handful of RV dealers nationwide that carry a wide variety of models and styles. It would be rare indeed (maybe impossible) to visit an RV dealership and be able to actually walk through all the floor plans available in any particular model.

In addition to dealers, there are numerous other sources of information available to you. I've already recommended that you take a year to do your research. Here are some information sources you can use.

> **Rallies and RV Shows**... A rally is a short term gathering of RVers that have some common goal or theme. An RV show allows dealers and manufacturers to bring in a variety of RVs so the public can see/tour them conveniently at one time and in one location. There are numerous shows and rallies for RVers and seminars are typically offered to the attendees. The

larger the rally, the greater the selection of seminar topics including maintenance, how-to, and various helpful hints.

"Fulltiming" (and certainly issues related to some aspect of fulltiming) is one of the relatively common seminar topics found at nearly every rally and many RV shows. However, just because someone is presenting a seminar does not mean they are the expert. Listen, question, and then ask around about the reputation of the presenter. Be especially careful if they are trying to sell a "Fulltiming Kit" or some such gadget. [Read more about Rallies and Shows in the section, *What Else Do We Need to Know.*] While unfortunate, occasionally, seminars turn into infomercials for some product that will supposedly solve your every problem. If the topic does not suit you, walk out. It's your time!

Books... There are a limited number of books available on fulltiming but many are now old. Unfortunately, a new "Edition" does not mean that the book was rewritten or even updated—maybe it was just reprinted! Some books now have the edition number changed for every printing—even if they are just reprinting

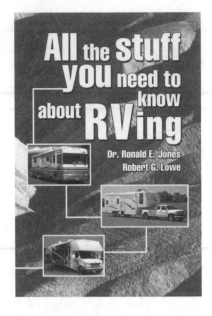

the original book containing all that old, original information. Certain information does not go out of date—some does. When we wrote *"All the Stuff...,"* I designed the content to not go out of date.

It seems logical that while all books should contain some helpful information, as a new or potential fulltimer, you will want the most current and correct information. The bad news... not all books are current nor are they correct. The technology changes rapidly. One example of this rapid change that is important to you is the growing number of campgrounds and other "hotspots" that offer a wireless Internet connection (WiFi)—free or paid.

Look over the books carefully and, if possible, read the copyright page for any original publishing dates (applying to copyright, printing, etc.). Call the publisher. If this doesn't help, carefully scan the book's content. One place to check for current content is any section on the Internet, WiFi, staying in touch on the road (cell phone air cards), or GPS systems as these are the newest, rapidly changing technologies. Any book not addressing or just casually mentioning these current topics may really be out of date.

Additionally, look for any mention of fuel prices as this will help you estimate when the book was actually written. The single most common topic that will "date" book content is any reference to prices. Photographs are also great tools for estimating the age of books. It is not uncommon to find ten-year-old information in books!

RV Magazines... Articles on fulltiming are common. Check online for back issues and you may be able to search for articles. Contact the editor and ask for copies of older articles. Be ready to question the information and use what fits and applies to you. It may also be possible to contact the writer or columnist directly to ask your questions. You will find that many of the recent RV magazines are often available at campgrounds for free. The campground laundry frequently does double duty as the book/ magazine exchange.

Online Groups... There are a number of groups online that focus on specific topics and "Fulltiming" is one of those. When you sign up, you will begin receiving e-mails sent by members of the group. These messages are their individual comments on some given topic that is under discussion at that time. You can elect to receive individual messages or highlights in a single message called a "digest." Some groups are very active with thousands of members and can generate hundreds of messages per day.

Join them, lurk (just watch and read) for a while to learn the focus of the group and more importantly, the "etiquette" of the group. Then, join their discussion at some point—ask a question or offer a comment (if you know what you are talking about). If you find that the focus of the group is not for you, you can always unsubscribe.

Online groups are made up of people with common interests and their experience can help you. Find these groups by contacting manufacturers, do a Google® search online, call RV organizations, ask dealers, ask other RV owners—it can be valuable and helpful information. However, online groups are simply a means for anyone to post their personal opinion to the group. Again, read carefully and verify your information. Remember, with online groups and forums, you can have amateurs answering questions.

Owner's Clubs... There are numerous clubs devoted to specific brands of RVs. These groups may have rallies (local, state, or national), newsletters, magazines, and on-line discussion groups. Their common focus is, obviously, on that specific brand of RV. If you have a used RV, often, you may actually be able to contact other owners of the model and year of the same RV you have. It is also a great method for finding out about problems and solutions specific to a particular coach and model year. Plus, you can often locate older technical manuals from some of the group members.

You are going to make a major life-changing decision that has both financial and personal value. Potentially selling a house and purchasing an RV would likely result in several-hundred-thousand-dollars worth of financial decisions. I always recommend that people do some serious research on decisions of this magnitude. Emotions aside, approach it like any business decision —carefully and methodically.

RV Organizations

There are literally hundreds (maybe thousands) of organizations, associations, and clubs for RVers. All of these are focused around the concept that a given group of RVers will have some common interest. Some groups are generic—they try to offer a large variety of services to virtually any type of RVer. Some will have a specific focus on a type of RV such as pick-up campers or motorhomes. Others focus on brands or even specific models of RVs—nearly every manufacturer sponsors a variety of "clubs" associated with their respective brand. Some are geographical. Many of the organizations (clubs) will have some annual dues but most are typically inexpensive. When you join, you get something, but do your homework. You may not need to join several.

I have included five different types here with the first two being the largest. I have belonged to the Good Sam Club and FMCA for many years and recently joined Escapees. I am familiar with S.M.A.R.T. and even though I qualify for membership, could not take advantage of their services—so I did not join. However, it has an excellent reputation. The last group is for women only and I do not qualify.

Good Sam… The Good Sam Club is one of the oldest, generic clubs for all RVers. Their membership is made up of owners of tent trailers to the largest motorhomes. The Good Sam Club provides nearly all services needed by RVers ranging from campground directories to emergency road service to rallies. They sponsor one of the largest rallies in the nation (called *"The Rally"*) attended by up to 4,000+ RVs. The Good Sam Club also has state rallies called "Samborees." Small chapter rallies take place all the time nationwide and even overseas.

The over one-million members receive an excellent magazine. *"Highways"* is for everyone. Members may then choose from two others:

- *"Motorhome"* magazine is designed for those RVers with drivable units
- *"Trailer Life"* is designed for RVers with towable units.

The Good Sam Club is a commercial entity operated by Affinity Group, Inc. Contact The Good Sam Club at 800-234-3450.

FMCA… The Family Motor Coach Association is specifically for drivable RVs—motorhome owners only. The organization has topped 400,000 members. Members receive the monthly magazine entitled *"Family Motor Coaching."*

FMCA sponsors two major "international" rallies every year and ten "Area" rallies around the nation. The "Areas" are made up of a number of states in some geographical location. The FMCA also sponsors a variety of specialty chapters ranging from "Discovery" (the motorhome model) owners to "100%ers" (those RVers living in their motorhome 100% of the time.) Contact FMCA at 800-543-3622.
<fmca.com>

S.M.A.R.T… This is the acronym for an organization named the "Special Military Active Retired Travel Club." S.M.A.R.T. is a nationwide, not-for-profit, veterans organization based on a common background of military service and an interest in the recreational vehicle (RV) lifestyle. Membership is made up of retired (pension-eligible) and active-duty travelers in any type of RV (motorhomes, travel trailers, 5th wheels, whatever). They have scheduled rallies—called "Musters,"—plus caravans, and other activities. Contact S.M.A.R.T at 800-354-7681.
<smartrving.net>

Escapees… Specifically focused on the fulltimer, Escapees (also known as "SKPs") is an organization providing information that helps the fulltimer. The Escapees also own and operate a series of campgrounds. The original (home) park is located in

Livingston, Texas. Escapees conduct rallies called "Escapades" and smaller gatherings called "HOPS." Members receive an excellent bi-monthly magazine entitled *"Escapees Magazine."* Contact Escapees at 888-757-2582.

<escapees.com>

RVing Women... An organization specifically for women RVers, their literature states that... "If you plan to travel by RV, already own one, or are just dreaming about your RV possibilities; if you are on the road full time or if you hung up your keys for whatever reason but want to stay connected to the women's RV network, we're here for you. We are a diverse group of women across the U.S. and Canada who enjoy RVing and love to travel."

They have rallies and chapter gatherings throughout the year plus a bi-monthly magazine entitled *"RVing Women."* Contact RVing Women at 888-557-8464.

<rvingwomen.org>

These organizations are a source of excellent information but you do have to dig it out. I always recommend joining for at least one year to enable you to receive and begin reading their magazines—long before you actually go. Then, continue your membership with those that offer you benefits specific to your RVing needs and wants. Many organizations will operate an online store where they also sell books and other merchandise.

How Much Will It Cost

Can We Afford To Do This

You will have different costs associated with fulltiming—some the same as living in a house and some different. Regardless, the cost of fulltiming is less than living in a house. That was our experience and many other fulltimers have confirmed that. Many told us that when they started fulltiming, their overall monthly cost-of-living decreased by 20–30% when compared to living in a house. Our personal cost-saving was close to 30%. Note that this is cash in hand, i.e., instant savings. It is money that you did not send/pay out at the end of the month.

What may be unique is that we have never had a fulltimer tell us their costs were higher than what they were paying in a house. However, if you moved out of a small, efficiency apartment into a $400,000 motorhome, eat out every meal, and only stay in resorts, you may find that your costs are higher, not lower. Typically, it's a less expensive way to live just as well.

Your personal cost-of-living is always based on your individual lifestyle. Some fulltimers radically change the way they do things. For example, if you rarely eat out now but start eating out most of  the time because you are fulltiming, your food costs will most likely increase significantly. Conversely, if you move your home-made RV to the desert and boondock, you can live pretty cheap! There's always the extreme. But for "normal" fulltimers, I believe it is valuable to know (within reason) your potential costs to help plan for the future.

Certainly, there is no way to predict, with accuracy, your cost savings without actually experiencing the lifestyle and tracking expenses. The best method to help visualize financial decisions is to use a simple spreadsheet to compare costs. Also, doing this will help eliminate surprises later on. To do this accurately, you need to know your current and actual cash-flow information.

Calculating Fulltiming Costs

I mentioned at the beginning of this book that we started fulltiming by accident. That's absolutely true. By coincidence and luck, I had decided I wanted to know our accurate costs to live in our house in preparation for that planned condo purchase (not for fulltiming in an RV). I simply wanted to understand the difference in cash flow based on our planned change in lifestyle (house-to-condo). With our accidental fulltiming, I was able to easily substitute the potential costs of RVing for the condo costs.

Sorry, but you will only be able to speculate (take a wild guess) at some of your fulltiming costs if you have little or no experience. We have included some potential costs in this book. However, costs change depending on the economy, geographical area, and lifestyle. Talk to other RVers, make some calls and ask about costs, read, join e-mail or online groups, and do the best research you can. First estimate and then carefully track your real fulltime RV costs when you start out. It will take some time to do this carefully and methodically. I suggest you approach it that way.

Some of you may be at an income level where consideration of costs will not be a factor in your decision. If so, the information (costs of fulltiming) will, at minimum, be interesting although not critical to your decision-making. However, most will have to factor this in to their overall decision.

> *A Personal Story… We decided knowing what it cost us to live in our house for one year would be helpful for planning a budget in preparation for any move. I went through the previous twelve months of bank statements, credit card statements, and cash receipts identifying expenditures **directly associated** with the house we had been living in for 16 years.*

For example, if we bought plant fertilizer—that went on the spreadsheet. If we purchased a lawnmower, that went on the spreadsheet, too. I even calculated the cost of the local newspaper delivery. Why? We paid for that newspaper because it was associated with living in that house at that time. We don't have that cost now.

Some have suggested that I should have amortized the lawnmower cost over several years—i.e., the life of the mower. I didn't because it was a true expense during that twelve-month period. If, for example, we had financed the cost longer than twelve months, I would have used the payments only during the one-year period. Conversely, if no lawnmower had been purchased, there would not have been any cost.

Carefully think through your expenditures and be sure to include everything possible. If you are the type that regularly pays cash for the odds and ends purchased for the house, you will have to devise your own method of researching and verifying those expenditures. The obvious goal is to put everything possible on that spreadsheet—i.e., if you spent money **directly associated** with the house, add it in. Doing this is not an attempt to "inflate" the housing expenses but to truly determine your costs of living there as accurately as possible. I am convinced people have no idea what it really costs to live in a house!

Comparing Apples to Kumquats

Sorry, you just cannot "ballpark" guess at the cost comparison of living in a house and an RV—it's really an unusual comparison. Plus, you cannot do this in "your head" since it will seem like you are comparing apples and oranges (or kumquats).

You must research costs carefully to be accurate and better understand what is involved. After all, you will benefit from the information. Here's one unusual example of comparing the cost of living in a house with the cost of fulltiming…

> When you rent a campsite for the night, you are actually paying for four things—electric, water, and sewer, plus a space to park your RV overnight. Sure, they may have a pool, cable TV, or other amenities but let's keep it simple. (Note: I believe the average campsite is now $25.00–$30.00/night out West and $45.00–$50.00/night in New England.) Compare this nightly campsite fee with the cost of living in your house for one night. (It's 2011, use $30.00 per night.)
>
> For the house, calculate the daily average cost of your electric, water, sewer, and heat. For accuracy, you must look at your real housing costs for the last 12 months (suppose you run a sprinkler or fill a pool in the summer). Add the costs for 12 months, divide by 365 (it's okay to use your calculator), and you have your daily average cost for those house utilities.
>
> For the RV, it may be a bit tricky figuring the cost of heat and hot water. For example…
>
> - If you have and use the combination heat pump/air conditioner (common on RV roofs), your heating cost is absorbed by the campground fees. Occasionally, campgrounds will charge extra for electricity but again, let's keep it simple.
>
> - If you use propane for heating and hot water, that cost is extra. Dig out your propane cost for your coach. (You need the last full year to accurately calculate your nightly cost.)

- Some motorhomes use the AquaHot® system where coach heat and hot water is heated by the fuel from the fuel tank (diesel). This is far more difficult to calculate.

Second (also more difficult), you need some housing expense with which to compare that campground-space rent. (Don't use your house payment because that equates to your RV payment.) I suggest using your property tax bill as a starting point. (Granted, this does not work for apartment dwellers unless you pay a "maintenance" or "association" fee.) Divide that annual tax bill by 365 to find a nightly average.

Next, add in yard work/maintenance costs. This may seem strange at first but you will not have this cost when fulltiming—the campground absorbs all this. Calculate what you spend to hire the yard work done or the cost of buying and operating the tools to do it yourself (lawnmower, snow blower, etc.). For apartment dwellers or condo owners, you may have a monthly maintenance fee that works here. Ultimately, you can calculate a pretty close average nightly cost for living in your house.

Remember my estimated average nightly campsite fee is $25.00–$30.00? How does that compare with the cost of living in your house for one night?

A Personal Story… When I originally estimated (budgeted) the fuel costs for us to fulltime, diesel fuel was actually selling at the pumps for $1.50/ gallon (seriously). To be on the "safe" side, I fudged the estimate an extra 10% and put in $1.65/gallon! Silly me.

While the previous exercise will provide a cost comparison for staying at a campground, it does not consider other house-related costs you no longer have to spend when fulltiming. For example, in your house, it is likely you have a standard phone—a "landline." It's been there forever and you pay for it each month. Even if you own the phone, you pay for their services.

You probably have a cell phone, too. When fulltiming, you will take the cell phone with you in the RV so those costs remain the same. However, you would actually get rid of the landline phone and service if you sold the house to start fulltiming. That is another example of unusual cost savings associated with fulltiming for RVers.

There are numerous other types of costs that are typically eliminated by fulltiming with some (like yard work) guaranteed to go away and some (like Internet) that may go away. These "normal" housing costs should go away…

- cable TV
- special movie channels
- leaf removal
- mowing
- snow plowing or cost of snow removal equipment
- trash pick-up
- all yard work and related tools and equipment
- cleaning service
- alarm systems
- the second car and its related costs (insurance, license, repair, maintenance, etc.)
- apartment/condo association dues

- local golf/country club dues
- property taxes
- swimming pool care and maintenance
- newspaper delivery

You may have others specific to your house. These too, must be considered to create some type of reasonably accurate budget. Unless you have a very large bank account, budgeting will be better than guessing!

The RV Purchase

The larger the RV the better, for most of us when fulltiming, because of storage capacity. You will occasionally run across fulltimers in a shorter Class A, Class C, or small travel trailer but they are definitely in the minority. Since the RV will be your "home," it may actually cost as much as a house. RVs are expensive. Plus, you must have some specific accessories based on your type of RV and then will choose others based on your personal requirements.

Where you want to go and stay may also affect your purchase decision. Currently, many/most state parks have a maximum size limitation of about 30–35 feet. Most of these campsites were developed years ago when RVs were smaller.

Do I Drive or Tow It

Whether you choose to drive the RV or tow it is, of course, a personal decision. I'm often asked what I recommend. This is difficult because I have no idea of your lifestyle. However, I do have some guidelines and some thoughts that may be helpful to you when trying to decide.

If you like to meander—i.e., spend a few days here, a week there, see the local sites, eat the local food—and move on to the next stop (30 or 300 miles), then I recommend a motorhome. It is the ideal vehicle for this type of travel. Plus you must drive a motorhome some specific amount each month to maintain the warranty and keep everything working. Just parking it for weeks or months will cause any vehicle to rapidly deteriorate.

If you like to get to your destination and stay several weeks or months, then a towable RV (5th wheel or travel trailer) is perfect. Arrive, set it up, and it's a great place to live with lots of storage and space. I've always considered a 5th wheel or travel trailer the perfect "snowbird" RV since they typically spend a few winter months in one location.

Motorhome Advantages and Disadvantages

There are two unusual advantages to having a motorhome. One, you can actually "set up"—at the campsite—without having to go outside. This,  of course, does not include hooking up to utilities. However, you can often level the coach, put out the slides, fire up the TV, fix dinner, and even go to bed for the night without stepping outside. You cannot do those things with a towable RV. This may become a significant advantage during a long and heavy downpour.

A second unusual advantage is the ability to drive away almost immediately—a factor in really bad or dangerous weather. Unhooking a motorhome and being ready to drive can actually be accomplished in about five minutes! I don't suggest doing it that quickly under normal circumstances as you will not have time to check thoroughly on everything. However, in a real emergency, you can drive away in a hurry.

Pro's to owning a motorhome...

- safety when driving since you sit up high and can see over normal cars and trucks
- the view out the front when parked
- full access to living area without going outside
- smoothest ride of any vehicle

Con's to owning a motorhome...

- higher initial cost—especially diesel pushers
- lower fuel economy—the larger the unit, the lower the mpg

Towable Advantages and Disadvantages

Many RVers in rural areas purchase a 5th wheel. They may already own a pickup that can pull some type of trailer. The addition of a hitch may be all they need thereby enabling them to keep their initial purchase costs low.

Pro's to owning a towable...

- only need to maintain one vehicle—the truck
- less overall and tire cost
- fuel economy (mpg) better than a motorhome.
- more of a "home-feeling"—bedroom at one end and kitchen/dining at the other

- more overall living length—none lost with dash
- higher ceiling height allows more upper storage, ceiling fans, etc.
- easier to store for the winter (no engines to start)
- can store longer.

Con's to owning a towable…

- the tow vehicle is larger and typically much harder to park in shopping centers, downtown, etc., than a toad (usually a car)
- backing a 5th wheel or trailer may be more difficult due to blind side
- some upscale RV "resorts" only allow motorhomes—no 5th wheels or trailers
- takes longer to hookup and unhook and get underway than a motorhome
- takes more time to level than a motorhome
- when traveling, no access to the fridge or bathroom without going outside
- the tow vehicle "ride" is usually rougher than a diesel-pusher motorhome.

The purchase of an RV is the major expense. Simply trading the payment on an RV for the payment on a house may be just a wash when estimating your fulltiming budget. Keeping the house plus paying for the RV can be expensive. If you try "justifying" the cost of buying an RV while keeping the house, you will likely go a bit crazy. It really can't be justified. If you keep the house, your cost of RVing will increase significantly due to the RV payment becoming an additional, not a replacement, expense.

New vs. Used

This is the classic conflict all RVers have to face—do I purchase a new or used unit? Simply, there is no answer but your answer. That is, what can you afford, what are your skills in having to possibly repair or rebuild one, what is your time frame, do you want to travel in it or work on it, does peace of mind count for anything, and on and on?

Purchasing a new coach does not ensure that everything works perfectly. It does ensure that the coach is under warranty and any repair costs are covered for a given period of time.

How Many Slides

Slides on any RV are now considered a necessity by many and, I must admit, they are a great convenience to fulltimers. We like ours and can't imagine being in a coach without slides. When our slides are in, we call it "living in hallway." But how many slides do you really need?

One of the consistent suggestions I offer in our seminars is this... a unit with multiple slides is the most adaptable, flexible, usable, livable unit. There is a good reason for this. That is, you can almost always gain some living space by putting out at least one slide in any parking situation.

Some of the older private campgrounds, most of the state parks, and lots of the national parks have smaller camp sites.

Smaller means that sites are both shorter and narrower. We have found that we could not put out various slides due to boulders, trees, posts, a cactus, concrete picnic tables, stumps, tree limbs, shore power poles, and the list goes on. With a multiple-slide RV, you have maximum flexibility because one will almost always go out, and with luck, two, three, or all of them. Every one gives you additional living space and makes staying there longer a far more pleasant experience. One thing to keep in mind... you do not gain any functional or usable space with any slide—only some extra space where you can walk around.

Here's one suggestion... be sure to check the RV before you purchase it to see if you can truly function normally with any/all slide configurations. Take several hours while looking at the RV and spend time in it with all possible slide configurations. This means checking to see if you could live in the RV with every combination of slides in and out. Don't just run the slide in and out but when they are in, can you get to your coffee pot, underwear, food, etc., can you sleep in the bed, and can you see the TV? Simply, is this RV fully usable all the time?

When slides are in the travel position on some RVs, you may not have access to certain things. I was told by one couple they looked at a motorhome that when the slides were in (travel mode), the entrance to the bathroom was blocked, i.e., no toilet! That wouldn't work for us.

Just Order One

You might consider ordering the RV of your dreams. If you are purchasing new, then ordering may give you some negotiating room (at this point, no one—you, the dealer, and manufacturer— has any money invested). Ordering an RV is a relatively smooth process. You do work with a dealer and sales rep but frequently may be in contact with the manufacturer.

Ordering an RV provides the opportunity to customize it to some degree. I recommend you keep this customization to a minimum to reduce additional costs—the goal here is not to try to redesign the RV. However, the customization can greatly increase your satisfaction with the layout or other aspects of the RV.

We have ordered two motorhomes. Our minor changes included moving the main electrical boxes out of the rear closet and into an upper cabinet in the bathroom. We also had them remove a three-drawer

cabinet that was literally sitting inside the rear closet. Doing this gave us an additional three feet of full-length hanging closet space —a lot in any RV. We did not want the toothbrush holder and soap dishes mounted in the bathroom. Plus, we did not want a window in the rear (short) wall of the front driver-side slide. To match the interior, this window would have required a wood lambrequin sticking out about four inches and interfering with the movement of one dining chair. It's great without that window!

Customization does not mean completely rearranging the floor plan. It does allow you to incorporate those custom touches that fit your lifestyle and make you a bit more comfortable in your RV. After all, we have never used a traditional toothbrush holder in any home we have lived in.

Find your manufacturer's schedule for the year. For example, lets assume that the first of next year's new models will be produced in August (yes, sometimes that early) so the changeover to the next year's model would likely start the following April. Order your RV to be ready in December or January. Why? The new-model "bugs" have been worked out of the current model-manufacturing process and the plant hasn't started tooling up for the next model year yet. You are more likely to get a "better" one.

RV Service On The Road

The process of getting service done on your RV is different especially if you are traveling. While you likely have experience scheduling and then having service done on your car, it's very different with an RV. There are three primary types of places that provide RV service...

- Dealers
- Factory service centers
- Mobile service technicians.

All of them can provide excellent service. All can be iffy. The main advantage to the factory service center is they typically have better access to more parts. The dealers may have to order parts and these are shipped in by various methods ranging from overnight delivery to someone paddling a canoe upstream. Another difference—but not an advantage—is that a dealer (an authorized service center for a specific brand of RV) generally must follow more "rules" than the factory service center. Rules include having to call the manufacturer for approval on some types of work—especially warranty work.

Whether a new or old RV, they all need service at some point. Assuming you cannot perform that work, the first step is to call for an appointment. Surprise! You may have to wait several weeks or months for an appointment. I called one (very large) dealer in October and was told they had just a few appointments left the following February! Seriously.

Plan (if you can) for this. If you are going to be on an extended trip and know you will need service at some specific time (for example, one year), then if possible, go ahead and schedule it. You can always cancel. The best time to get the unit serviced is before you store it for the winter, not when you pull it out of storage and want to leave on that big trip next week.

What about needing an emergency repair? "Emergency" service will get you in the door in, maybe, 2-3-4 days. Emergency service is generally defined as any work required to continue to actually use/live in the RV (water, electrical, driving/towing or safety problems). You may even need a motel during this time. Cosmetic or numerous other issues (regardless of your perception of "serious") are not considered emergencies. These range from paint scratches to your microwave not working.

Patience is the answer... When you arrive for service, patience is your only answer. It will generally be slow and they may not even start on your coach for a day or two. One reason for this is that the people who show up for service, come with an additional list of things that they need done. Sure, they had a repair list when they called and made the appointment but they show up with another list—those things that stopped working between their initial call and actual appointment. This "second" list can become quite lengthy especially if there was a long lead time when making the appointment.

The service center will estimate the time needed to do the work from your first list and allocated that time for you. Let's assume they estimated three full days to do all your repairs and set your service appointment for a Monday. When you show up, you casually mention that "By the way..." and show them fifteen other items that now need fixing, too. For my example, let's assume it would take two more days to complete the work on that second list. If the service center agrees to do everything (both lists), you are there for a week.

The problem lies in that if they have another coach scheduled for that Thursday—your original work was to be finished on Wednesday. The "Thursday" person is now pushed forward until the following Monday! And that is assuming they really do get you out of there on Friday. When you multiply this type of problem by 10 or 30 or 50 service bays, it becomes overwhelming. Patience is the answer.

If you are getting your work done under an "extended warranty" contract, then **you must follow protocol** established by that insurance company. Most require you to call and receive approval **PRIOR** to the work being started. Your service center will need to know if you are planning to use an extended warranty to help pay the costs. They may help you with the call, can explain the nature of the planned work/service, and can discuss the time estimated on the various repairs. Communication between the service center, the extended warranty company, and you will help eliminate problems with final payment for service.

Accessories—Necessary Expenses

If you now have an RV, you already have many of the required accessories. Buying an RV (your first one or if its been several years since you owned one) will require you to purchase certain accessories—some are expensive.

Necessary RV Accessories

Here are a few that are (almost always) required but the first two are a must if you want to tow a car with a motorhome...

- **Tow Bar**. You must have a tow bar, a car dolly, or a trailer. All are expensive—easily in the $1,000 range.

- **Supplemental Braking System**. If you tow a vehicle, this is a device designed to apply the brakes in the car when you apply the brakes in the motorhome. A supplemental braking system is legally required in most states and all the Canadian provinces. Can you get by without one? Probably, but if you have an accident where one is required… well, enough said. The cost is about $1,000.

- **RV Insurance**. You must have insurance. The bank will likely require it if you have the RV financed. There are a number of companies that insure RVs. I always suggest using a company in the business of insuring RVs as opposed to one that, while they may sell you insurance, really does not know that aspect of the business. Insurance costs are widely varied based on the RV itself.

- **Emergency Road Service**. One common type of special RV insurance is called "Emergency Road Service." It is designed to provide financial assistance, technicians, or professional help for minor emergencies while you are using the RV. (See the Chapter entitled *"Emergency Road Service"* for a detailed explanation.) I highly recommend this and have used it on occasion. It is inexpensive—often less than $100.00 per year.

- **Campground Directory**. There may be RVers out there without campground directories but I don't know any of them. These inexpensive books are invaluable for finding campgrounds where you want to stay. Then, you call and make the reservation to lock in your site and dates. Yes, this information is on the Internet but that is sometimes difficult to access driving down the highway. Some directories are also available on CDs and are searchable. There are specialized directories, too. For example, there is a U.S. Military Campground directory for active and retired military. Membership campgrounds will publish their own directories. You may actually end up carrying three or four different directories. This information is also online.

Nice-To-Have RV Accessories

The items in this category make your life and especially RV-related activities easier, safer, more efficient, or more fun. With that, my consistent recommendation is that you should use the RV a while before you buy anything including stuff in my list below. One exception is that Motor Carrier's Atlas—when you need it, you really need it!

Consider the following:

- **GPS**. It's really handy to know where you are and how to get where you are going. The best GPS for motorhomes is one running on a laptop or an iPad. Their screen displays are 4–5 times larger than postcard-sized screens found in car units. Visit <**aboutrving.com**> for a major article on the advantages of using the iPad as a GPS.

  Regardless of what you paid for that GPS, the maps are constantly going out of date. It is estimated that the roads (highways) change by 10% every two years—new routes, bridges, entrances, street names, etc. If you can update your maps, great, do it. If you cannot, after a couple of years, think about investing in another unit.

- **Tire Pressure Monitor.** A device that constantly monitors all tire pressures and sends that information to a receiver on the dash. They will provide a warning sound with a sudden loss in tire pressure.

- **Two-way Radio.** Two-way communication for pilot and co-pilot. This can be a hand-held radio or a headset.

- **Digital Video Recorder.** A device for recording TV shows. The DVR replaced the video tape recorder. The DVR allows you to watch your favorite shows and fast-forward through the commercials—a good thing.

- **Satellite Dish.** A popular system with which to access the Internet and TV is the satellite dish. Many of the systems are automatic (Find and  Stow with a single button), may use a single "dish" for both TV and Internet, and are reasonably fast speeds (far better than the dial-up modem).

- **Sun Screens.** Window coverings to prevent sun's rays from entering the RV and privacy.

- **Motor Carrier's Atlas.** Buy it at any truck stop and get great information very applicable to RVers in both the USA and Canada. The Motor Carrier's Atlas contains all the low bridge clearance locations in the USA and Canada. Remember, you drive or pull a really tall vehicle and there are bridges you cannot drive under.

The Motor Carrier's Atlas also contains toll-free (800) phone numbers for all states and provinces to get up-to-date...

    A. Road Construction info

    B. Weather info

    C. General Information... from the state/ provincial police (a non-emergency number for any questions regarding driving in that specific state or province).

Interestingly, the maps aren't very good for RVers since the truck routes are heavily highlighted. This highlighting blocks other information that RVers may need—this may be good for truckers, but not for you. Buy a cheap "normal" road atlas, too, for the maps. Upgrade the normal atlas every year. The Motor Carrier's Atlas is good for 3–4 years since government agency phone numbers are pretty stable.

- **Washer/Dryer**. Get a combo unit—a washer and dryer in one single unit. They work and work well for the space consumed. There can be lots of wrinkles with these units unless you learn the secrets of how to use them. They are different from your home set or those at a laundromat.

  Purchase a copy of *"Wrinkle-Free RV Laundry"* (ISBN 978-156870-590-3) to learn all the secrets of using the combo washer/dryer. Available at
  <aboutrving.com>

  We do not recommend the stacked washer and dryer for three reasons. First, some brands/ models require you to be plugged into 50-amp service. If you are in a campground with only 30-amp power available (and they are very common), you cannot use your washer and dryer. Second, the stacked units consume double the amount of space—critical storage space in any size RV. Third, stacked units do not automatically solve the wrinkle problem.

- **Extended Warranty**. I am usually not in favor of extended warranties on anything. However, RVs have so many unusual and expensive "systems" and items that I have purchased an extended warranty in the past. On my last three

Class A coaches, two had extended warranties. An extended warranty is nothing more than insurance. It's great if you need it but otherwise, you are just paying for nothing.

Extended warranties for motorhomes are purchased for miles **and** time. For example, 50,000 miles or 48 months—whichever comes first. You will have to estimate/guess at your driving habits to best determine what would work best for you.

RV Parks or Campgrounds

One major and ongoing cost of RVing is the fee you pay for a place to park your RV overnight and hook up to their utilities—i.e., commonly called your "campground fee." It is common for RVers to choose to only stay one night at a location while traveling en-route from point to point. It is also common for other RVers to stay several months at one location—this is typical of the classic "snowbird" who spends several winter months in the warm south and then returns to the north. Regardless, unless you own the site or it's free, you must pay to rent it.

There are four types of places for RVs to park overnight or longer for a fee: campgrounds, RV parks, RV resorts, and mobile home parks. Consider this brief comparison…

Campgrounds… This term is applied to just about every type of paid "camping" facility whether it accommodates an RV or not. Campgrounds may allow tent camping. All campgrounds do not have utility hookups for RVs—especially those in state or national parks. Many campgrounds (continued p 46)

Note the close parking here. The lamp fixture (above) is tucked into the corner of the slide. Below, the other side is within inches of the green utility stand. Sometimes you just have to make it fit.   (W. David Greer Photo)

are older—again, in state or national parks—or the classic "Mom and Pop" campground built 30-40-50 years ago. The large RVs manufactured today may not conveniently fit into some of those campsites and you may not even be able to drive through the campground due to trees, overhanging limbs, tight corners, and crowded conditions.

A Personal Story… We had been away from RVing for several years but were on our first big trip in our new Class A. I called the reservation number for the National Park Service and asked if we could get into Yellowstone Park for one night only. We wanted to drive through the park heading north to Montana but had to stay somewhere.

The person told me there was one site left that was big enough for our coach—at the time, a 39-foot Bounder motorhome. It was a "primitive" site (no hookups) but he assured me we would fit. We went in.

The camp host nearly had a stroke when he saw our rig. I told him our site number. He rode his bicycle up to see the site. Then, he guided me the only way into the site by taking a loop road the wrong way while his wife stopped traffic the other direction. We fit, but barely. We managed to put our slides out on one side.

Leaving the next day, the pines did a great job of dusting off my coach while getting out of there, again, going the wrong way. Never again!!!

RV Parks... Typically, these commercial ventures are set up to accommodate RVs for overnight stays or longer and will likely have some utilities—50-amp at best but 30-amp is also common. Sometimes these parks are older and sites may be a bit small for today's huge RVs. "Small" means both length and width. I like to check it out by actually going back to the site before committing to it. Pace it off if you think it's too short for your rig.

RV Resorts... Ideally, resorts are built around the concept of long-term stays and may offer unique amenities (golf, exercise rooms, swimming pools, tennis courts, and spas, for example). True resorts may also offer RV sites for sale. These resorts will almost always be more expensive on their nightly rate than parks or campgrounds.

The problem is that you may not be able to "trust" the name so be prepared to ask detailed questions. The name "Resort" does not automatically mean that an RV park or campground is some big, modern facility laid out to accommodate any size RV.

Mobile Home Parks... These parks were definitely set up for long-term rental spaces with the giant mobile homes permanently set in place. Some may have RV spaces for rent. We have stayed in several and they were all fine. Most are basic (a few amenities such as a pool) but the nightly fee was appropriate.

Campground Rates

During 2007, we paid for camping a total of 221 nights. That included about two months of travel in western Canada plus all over the USA with the exception of the southwest and New

England. Our tracked costs indicated an average expense of about $25.00 per night for campground rental. In 2010, I estimated an average nightly cost of $35.00 out West, $30.00 in the midwest and $40.00–$45.00/night up the East coast and in New England. Or, if you need a "best-guess" nationwide average, use $30.00 per night.

If we take an average nightly campground cost of $30.00, that calculates to $900.00/month for rent if you stay 30 nights and pay the full nightly rate. However, most campgrounds will have a reduced rate for weekly, monthly, or longer stays. The exception to this is during peak season or specific holidays. There are various "deals" such as "Pay for 2 nights and stay 3," or "Pay for 6 nights and stay 7." I've even seen "Pay for three weeks and stay a month." Regardless, the deals are available so be sure to ask.

It is not uncommon to find a monthly rate at 55–60% off the nightly rate—including all utilities. During February/March 2010, we stayed at a "normal" (no frills) campground for one month in

Georgia. Our site had 50-amp, water, and sewer at a total cost of $328.00 for the month. That is inexpensive rent and utilities—an average of slightly below $11.00 per night. There were no amenities (pool, etc.) but that's fine with us as we do not use them anyway.

Check the price carefully since some parks have a reduced monthly rate but then you must pay additional for your electric. Your actual nightly cost will average higher than the quoted nightly camping fee when you add on your electric costs. Some parks will add a daily fee for electric (I have paid $2.00 per day. I have seen $3.00 per day.) for short-term (1 or 2 days) stays. In addition to the rent, other parks will actually read the electric meter at the site monthly and bill you for the electricity used. Often, the electric is marked-up by the park.

Other mark-ups may apply and you may be charged for a variety of things. I have seen extra charges for washer/dryers, air conditioners, pets, children, more than 2 adults in the coach, cable TV, WiFi, and Internet. You must call and ask the questions. Think of it like a larger purchase—are you getting what you want for the price you want to pay? This is especially critical with snowbirds who may be staying 3–4 months in one park. You need to know your costs up front if you want to budget accurately.

Campground Discounts

Membership Campgrounds... There are a number of membership campgrounds—resorts/parks—some of the parent companies are quite large and include several hundred member-parks. These memberships may be purchased for a fee (sometimes in the thousands of dollars) and then you can use any of the respective parks (exclusively) for free or a reduced nightly/weekly fee. There may also be limits to the time you can stay in one park.

My recommendation is that you approach this like any "business" deal. That is, if it will pay for itself in savings (really save you money within a reasonable amount of time), then it may be a good purchase decision. For new fulltimers, I always recommend that you travel for a year or two before making a decision this costly. Your lifestyle may actually change through your newfound freedom. You will discover new ways to enjoy your time.

Discount Campgrounds... There are numerous discount programs for campgrounds. and several companies offer discounted camping. You sign up for some annual fee (usually less than $100) and when you stay at one of "their" member campgrounds, you may get a discount—but it's not guaranteed!

The typical arrangement is that when you pay your membership fee, you get a directory of their member campgrounds and it is usually available online. When you call for a reservation, you always ask if they honor the discounts. If "yes" and if a discounted site is available, you can overnight for a reduced campground fee—usually 50%.

The tricky part is that they all have different "rules." For example, the discount may apply to just the first night, not on the weekend, only on Tuesdays, or the first three nights, and on and on. You have to call and ask. Get specific with them on what and how much will be discounted. Interestingly, we have used one of these discount companies and our best consistent savings was in Canadian campgrounds traveling through the Maritimes. They sort of tossed out the "rules" and just discounted the sites.

Campground Discounts for Everyone... Most campgrounds have smaller discounts—commonly 10%. This is based on your having a membership in some organization whether RV-related or otherwise including the common RV organizations such as the Good Sam Club and FMCA, AAA, AARP, and others. These campgrounds are so common you can pay your membership dues from your savings over time. It's your money. Just ask.

My strong recommendation is that you **not purchase any discount camping programs** (no matter how cheap) until you know they will work for you. You can easily determine this on a "normal" trip by asking any campground you call if they are a membership or discounted campground. If they say yes, then keep track of this accumulated potential savings. If you find that you could have saved money (and paid for the cost of the membership) over some reasonable time, then it could be a good deal for you prior to your next extended trip. However, only experience will determine this.

Work "Kamping" or Trading Labor for Space

I previously mentioned "work camping." This is when RVers trade their labor for a campsite. National and state parks plus private campgrounds commonly offer seasonal work-camping opportunities including maintenance, running the office, working in the gift shop, or being a camp host.

Work Kamping is one source of temporary employment unique to RVing that could help defray the cost of staying longer in any one location. [Author note... If you look for this topic online, try searching for "Work Kamping" with a "K" and/or a "C," and "Workamping."] Campgrounds offer work-camping opportunities for as short as a week. Other campgrounds want you on site for the season (whatever that length of time might be but defined as their "local" season). Requiring a contract for a specific amount of time is common especially among the larger campgrounds.

Some campgrounds will trade you a space for as few as ten hours of work, per week, per person. What this means is that for less than two days work you have a free campsite with full hook-ups. If your days are scheduled together, this gives you five days a week for sightseeing and getting to know the area.

Another type of work camping is to be a hired employee. You are paid a salary and your campsite is part of the pay. Usually the pay is minimum wage. Some campgrounds pay more, especially if you have been there for more than one season or have special skills.

Lots of campgrounds are looking for individuals with special skills such as electrician, plumber, computer technician, carpenter, etc. to help improve their parks. This can be a good way to keep up your skills and make some money in the process. Work camping is not for everyone, but is a viable option, especially if you are on a tight budget.

Now, a really special thing that work camping gets you— especially with the variety of national parks—is a unique place to stay. Mostly, you stay in the park and therefore, have some "back door" access that normal visitors do not. That could be a unique experience and worth something.

Tourist or Campground Destination

There are many types of RVers. Each individual will find the kind of RVing that suits them best. Some prefer to be on the move on a fairly constant and regular basis—we do this—we meander. Still others prefer staying in one place longer and getting a real feel for the local area.

Some RVers really function like tourists and primarily travel for the sights and places to visit with disregard for what camping facilities are available. They will plan to travel to a city, national park, a geographical area (e.g., the Canadian Maritimes), or some tourist place and then look for a campground close by to provide easy access to their destination. We travel in this manner.

One example is that we recently decided to visit Vancouver, British Columbia and then found a campground close to the city. We were there for a week, it was great access, and we only had a short drive into the city. Another time, we wanted to visit the Rock and Roll Hall of Fame in Cleveland. We looked for a campground close in and made our reservation. Both examples are tourist destinations.

Even when traveling long distances, for example, with no firm plans to stop and be a tourist along the way, we still do not have predetermined campground destinations. We will drive until some point where we think we would like to stop in another hour or two. Then we locate a campground (or boondocking place) about an hour or two ahead of us, call, and go there (with permission or a reservation). This process allows us to stop when we want to rather than being forced to drive to a predetermined destination.

Other RVers plan their final destination around a specific campground. This is a prevalent practice with the membership campgrounds—the campground literally becomes the destination and whenever tourist activities are within a reasonable distance, great.

We do not travel in this manner. However, it seems that this could become somewhat unsafe. For example, suppose you are traveling across the nation and you have identified a specific campground where you want to spend the night—let's assume it's one of your nicer membership parks. You have made your reservation. But now you are tired of driving, the sun is in your face (think of that big RV windshield heading west in late afternoon), it's hot, and it's another 50 or 100 miles to your reserved campground. Do you keep driving? The answer, of course, is yes, you most likely do.

Doing that creates the potential to be somewhat dangerous. Friends have told us that if you cannot make it to a membership park for your reservation, a call is usually enough to delay your arrival for a day and, at the discretion of the park, they may waive any "no-show" charge.

Additionally, forcing yourself to drive to a campground destination may increase your costs. Suppose, for example, that your destination campground is 14 miles off your route. In a motorhome getting 7 miles per gallon and paying $3.50/gallon for fuel, that makes the additional driving cost of going there plus returning to your route a total of $14.00. That, plus the initial cost of the campground, would increase your total costs. We elaborate on this in the next section on "Fuel."

Temporary Destinations (Boondocking)

An instant, excellent, and fun method to save significant campground fees is to boondock (dry camp). Your RV is self-contained—you have everything needed on board for living comfortably without hooking up to utilities every night. You do not have to deprive yourself nor do without anything when boondocking. Plus, learning to boondock provides you with the convenience of being able to stop just about anywhere and at any time. See the chapter entitled *"Boondocking"* for information on living comfortably without depriving yourself of the comforts of home.

The cost savings through boondocking can be significant. Based on an average nightly campground cost of $30.00, if you **average boondocking just one night per week, that is an annual savings of $1,560** ($30.00 x 52 weeks = $1,560) or at $45.00, **an annual savings of $2,340!**

Boondocking is a great method for instantly saving money. For example, we averaged boondocking 11 nights per month in 2006 and 12 nights per month in 2007–2010. That calculates to 2.75 nights per week on average. Let's multiply (2.75 X $1,560 = $4,290 or 2.75 X $2,340 = $6,435) and by boondocking an average of just 12 nights per month, our annual savings of $4,290–$6,435 was significant. This savings, like the results from driving slower, is instant because you actually keep the money in your pocket. As other related costs continue to increase, certainly any potential savings approaching $5,000 is something to seriously consider.

Primarily, we boondock basically for convenience. Of course, we realize the savings, too. At the end of the year, we total our real campground costs and then divide by 365 to get a true average nightly cost. For 2006, our average nightly cost was $12.21. 2008 was $13.83, and 2009 was $16.72. This included paying for a few nights (on the ocean) at $90.00 per night down to zero (the cost of boondocking).

> **Try this:** If you are going to track your costs in a spreadsheet, identify those nights you actually boondock even though there is no cost. This will ensure that you account for every night of the year. Use a simple entry such as *"Boondock, Wal-Mart, Abilene, TX"* or *"Boondock, I-10 rest area, mm 265, TX."* Doing this will also help you track your progress. Remember the spreadsheet rule... Always make the description clear enough to help you recall it accurately three years from now in the IRS audit.

Fuel

Everyone gets excited about the cost of fuel (gas or diesel) and certainly it rates the most media attention. However, try thinking about fuel costs from a different perspective. Saving fuel is a second method for instantly saving money and there are no gadgets or magic fuel pills involved!

> **For example**... Let's assume you had planned and were willing to take that nationwide trip when fuel was $3.00/gallon. Now, it's $4.00/gallon and you can't afford that much!

> Think differently about fuel costs. You were ready to go and even willing to pay $3.00/gallon so now your **increased** cost is just $1.00 per gallon. All you need is

to figure out how to save the equivalent of $1.00 per gallon and you will have met your original budget.

Yes, I truly wish we could go back to those cheap fuel prices as shown above—but it's not likely to happen There are lots of ways to save on fuel and you get to actually pocket your savings instantly. First, think about living in a house. What other items ran on fuel that you no longer have to buy—second car, lawnmower, boat, etc. Some expenditures are simply a trade-off. I cannot speculate on your savings here but you can, based on your lifestyle. For example, track your fuel cost for that second car.

Second, it's easy to reduce your fuel costs up to about a 15% savings! The biggie... *Slow Down*. Reducing your highway speed from 65/66 mph to 55/56 mph will save approximately 15% in fuel consumption. This is not hard to do and is instant savings.

A Personal Story... In 2004/2005, I collected accurate engine data on fuel consumption for our Monaco Dynasty. We crossed the nation a couple of times so geography was not a consideration. All driving was with cruise control when possible. Without question, the major factor in saving fuel is highway-driving speed. Here are my real numbers:

16,419 miles @ 65/66 mph = 7.0 mpg

6,524 miles @ 60/61 mph = 7.4 mpg = saving 5.7%

*1,371 miles @ 55/56 mph = 8 mpg = **saving 14.3%***

Doing this creates instant savings, it's something available to everyone (at no extra cost), and ensures your ability to RV more and farther for the same costs. Plus, there are several other hints and tricks you can do that will also result in saving fuel costs. Consider this...

- Lighten the load. We carry too much stuff. Make a list of things you rarely use and remove them. While you may be proud of your horseshoe or brick collection, don't carry all of them with you. Just take your prize brick! It's okay to carry pictures of the rest of the collection.

- Unless you are boondocking for several days, never travel with a full tank of fresh water. For the day or overnight trip to the campground, a 1/4 tank is usually plenty.

- Reduce engine idling time.

- Keep your vehicle tuned and serviced regularly.

- Keep your tires properly inflated.

- Don't forget your tow vehicle—tire pressure, load, and cleanliness are a factor here, too.
- Plan to drive the RV fewer miles on your trip.
- Plan for longer side trips in the car.
- Wash your vehicles. Dirt on the surface creates drag and decreases air flow.

- Dump the gray and black (if more than 1/2 full) before you depart.
- Reduce the time you run your generator. For example, don't charge your batteries to 100%, take them to 90%.
- Weigh your motorhome (each wheel position), adjust your load, and set the correct tire pressure.
- Boondock. Every night you park at no-cost will save you approximately $30.00 in campground fees.

Except boondocking, all these positively affect your fuel consumption. Don't dismiss them as too minor to mess with. While any one of them may not be measurable by you (in terms of how much fuel they actually save), there is a positive, cumulative effect. Hey, it's your money!

An unusual but real fuel-saving tip... Assuming you know your real mileage (not the number you tell your friends), calculate driving costs to campgrounds in out-of-the-way places. (We used this example before.)

Your destination campground is 7 miles off your route. In a motorhome getting 7 miles per gallon and paying $3.50/gallon for fuel, that makes the additional driving cost of going there plus returning to your route a total of $7.00. You must add that $7.00 to the cost of your campground (it's the only reason you drove that 14-mile round trip). The result... that $20.00 "bargain" campground actually cost you $27.00. Now, is it worth it?

A fuel-rebate tip... Carry and use a credit card that provides cash back for fuel purchases. At present, most rebates are limited to 5% of some maximum dollar amount of charges. However, that is a direct savings and one more method for lowering your overall fuel costs. Call the card companies and ask.

Note: Watch the rebate cards for a maximum fuel purchase amount. Some pumps limit you to a maximum of $75.00. With a big diesel pusher, stop the pump just below $75.00, stop the pump, pay, and then reinsert the card and start again. It's a pain but it works. Just think, 5% of $4.00/gallon fuel saves you 20-cents per gallon and makes the fuel actually cost $3.80/gallon. Every 5% helps!

Remember our example at the beginning of this fuel-savings section? You were willing to travel at $3.00/gallon but can't afford $4.00/gallon. With the instant 15% savings by just slowing down, $4.00/gallon fuel becomes $3.40 ($4.00 X .85 = $3.40)! You're getting close! With slowing down plus getting the extra 5% rebate from the fuel card, $4.00/gallon fuel becomes $3.20 ($4.00 X .80 = $3.20)! You're getting closer!!!

Food

Food costs are determined by eating in or out and this is so personal that it does not warrant suggestions. It is, however, a cost and unfortunately, one that adds up daily. I suggest you plan to track this cost and don't casually dismiss it on the assumption that you have to eat whether you live in a house or RV.

Yes, we all have to eat but you will likely find that your "style" of eating changes when fulltiming. For example, you may find that you are eating more seafood because you happen to be traveling close to the ocean. You may find farmer's markets in abundance in one area and ethnic foods in another. For example, when you drive across Louisiana, you will find gumbo on nearly every menu! Simply, your eating style may change because of where you are. If this happens, your food costs will also change. Interestingly, those costs may increase or decrease and it is impossible to predict.

Cooking in an RV is easy and efficient. You can cook virtually anything in a modern RV that you can in a house with one exception—broiling. Many RVs now have the combined convection/microwave and, well, broiling is a challenge. Simply stated, it's much easier to broil in a normal household oven with a built-in broiler. You will find yourself cooking with fewer pots due to the RV cook surface—it just won't accommodate multiple large pots and pans.

Fulltiming will create two situations that will help (or sort of force you) to reduce your food costs—but in a good way. First, is the limited storage space in the RV. You do not have room to store the multiple packages or cans of food nor do you have freezer space and therefore, your buying patterns must change. One example is that you will have to stop "bulk" shopping. Even if that dozen cans of chicken soup is on sale at a great price, you will not have storage space. Also, you will not be able to purchase those unusual food items and store them "just in case" you want to try some recipe in the future. There's just not room. It's fine to try that new recipe, but go purchase the unusual ingredients when you need them.

> *A Personal Story...* I do most of our cooking and
> have for many years. I am a kitchen experimenter
> and love to try new recipes. When we were in our
> house several years ago, there was some recipe
> that called for a spice called "Beau Monde." I
> bought the spice, fixed the dish, and we did not
> care for it. However, I kept that bottle of Beau
> Monde but never used it again. I had to give it up
> when we moved into our coach.

The second situation is that assuming you keep the typical array of stuff in your fridge, there is little (or almost no) space for storing leftovers, in the fridge or in the freezer. Therefore, you will have to purchase and prepare foods in quantities that (hopefully) will be consumed in one sitting. Even the typical RV-style fridge in larger RVs will have limited space—not close to that normal household unit. Some larger motorhomes are now using the all electric "household" style fridge. These units are larger than the typical RV-style fridge.

The same applies to the RV pantry/food storage area. There is less room for dry or canned food storage than you find in a house. While you may be accustomed to having a wide selection of foods at your disposal, that likely will not be the case in an RV.

Eating out more often is common among RVers. Local restaurants are often excellent, low cost, and unique. You can spend any amount eating out. In areas where there are large numbers of senior citizens, you will often find the "early" dinner discounts. Generally, these smaller-portioned-full-meals are served between 4:00 and 6:00 PM and the cost savings is significant. Rallies and RV parks will often have a potluck food gathering scheduled. It's the classic "bring a dish" and join in the meal. These types of gatherings will also reduce food costs.

Maintenance

You will have maintenance costs and will need to plan/ budget for them. The older the RV, typically the more you have to do yourself or spend to have it done. Repair costs in an RV are never inexpensive plus with the number of different systems (from a diesel engine to a microwave oven), no one place is going to be the "expert" on everything. Ongoing preventive maintenance will help eliminate some costly repair and, even worse, downtime. Downtime, i.e., being stuck at some dealership waiting for repair or parts, is not much fun. For any particular type and model of RV, I always recommend the following...

- Talk with the manufacturer (their tech support can answer lots of questions).

- Visit and tour their factory and, if possible, watch your model of RV actually being built.

- Find an "Owner's Rally" and attend. Nearly every seminar will focus on your type and model of RV. Even OEM's like battery or generator manufacturers may be there with a seminar or vendor booth. Plus, the opportunity to interact with other owners is invaluable.

- OEMs (Original Equipment Manufacturers) have preventive maintenance information. For example, the tire manufacturers have brochures on RV weight, weighing individual wheel positions, tire pressure, load balancing, etc. Call them direct and ask for information.

- Nearly all the RV magazines will have regular articles on maintenance.
- Many RV websites will offer a maintenance section or articles.
- Join an "Owners" e-mail or online group. I'm most familiar with Bounder owners and Monaco owners. These groups offer every level of expertise and can offer advice for nearly any RV-related problem—no matter how obscure.
- Many of the Owner's Clubs often have a monthly or bi-monthly newsletter—often containing maintenance tips. It is definitely worth the small annual dues.

Miscellaneous

There are lots of "extra" costs when traveling and while you cannot plan for most of them, you need to be aware they exist. For example, we love museums—especially the small ones that are sort of hidden in many of the small towns nationwide. We walked in the dinosaur tracks at Dinosaur Valley State Park in Texas. We stumbled onto the Charles M. Schulz Museum and visited Snoopy and Charlie Brown. In Pecos, Texas, we found the "West of the Pecos Museum" with original bullet holes from the gunfights! All required an entrance fee—not any significant amount—but it is a miscellaneous cost associated with RVing. Two people, paying an $8.00 entrance fee, once per week, is an annual cost of $832.00 ($8.00 x 2 = $16.00 x 52 = $832.00). If your budget is important, be aware of these costs.

Another hidden cost is toll roads and ferries. They are considerably more expensive for a motorhome towing a car or a vehicle towing an RV. Usually, you are charged by the number of axles or length. With our motorhome and car, we have five axles.

The cost of taking two vehicles on board a ferry—with one of them oversized—is considerably more than the cost of a single vehicle. With a motorhome, you may be able to reduce your fees if you unhook and drive both vehicles onto the ferry. That, of course, is not an option if you tow your RV.

> *A Personal Story... We were taking the ferry from Port Angeles, Washington to Victoria, on Vancouver Island, British Columbia. I was told by the northbound ferry-terminal crew that it would be less expensive if I kept the motorhome and car together. I did. It was. Upon our return a week later, I was told by the southbound ferry-terminal crew that it would be less expensive if I unhooked the car. I did. It was. Who knows why?*

Make the Decision

What's Next

So, you've finally made the decision. If "Yes," then great. There's work to do to get ready. If it's a "No," then give this book to someone who is thinking about fulltiming. It's a great gift and they will appreciate it.

With that "Yes" decision, the more lead time you have to actually get ready—i.e., prepare, do your research—is better. If you have a year or at least several months, there will be much less chaos in getting ready. Remember our story, *"Fulltiming by Accident,"* at the beginning of the book? We pulled it off in three weeks but already owned a motorhome and had the experience of using one. However, we did not have any real experience fulltiming, but any experience helps a bit.

Interestingly enough, getting your mail changed is one of the longest and most difficult to accomplish. It's easy to find a mail forwarding service (we discuss these services later in the book under the heading *"Regular Mail"*) and it's certainly easy to have the U.S. Post Office forward your mail.

The U.S. Post Office will do a "Temporary Forwarding" for one year. For a "Permanent Forwarding," they will forward your mail for one year and then for the next six months, return any mail to the sender with your new address on it. I recommend you have any mail forwarding service in place and working for at least two months prior to leaving. This will provide the opportunity to test it.

I recommend you make an effort to stop receiving heavy things like catalogs. These may result in a significant cost to mail-forward them simply due to weight. The next heavy item is magazines. With these, you may want to stop some and keep others. Think carefully about those activities you may not be doing because you will be RVing (traveling). For example, maybe your monthly *"Country Gardening"* magazine should be stopped if you are not going to garden for at least a year. You can always start receiving it again and in the meantime, you can buy the latest issue. Keep in mind, any subscriptions you have cancelled can always be started again.

What Do We Do With Our Stuff

Everybody has stuff. To quote George Carlin, "A house is just a pile of stuff with a cover on it." You must do something with at least part of your stuff if you plan to fulltime. Storage buildings are everywhere and available at a cost. Controlled-climate (air conditioned and heated) storage is always best since photographs, adhesives (virtually all furniture—antiques, too—is partially glued together), and other assorted things are generally better off stored in controlled conditions. Extreme heat and cold will destroy your stored items so be careful. If you live in the far north or south, this is a major consideration.

Don't just cram your stuff in someone's garage regardless of the cost savings. While a good-hearted neighbor, friend, or even a family member may offer their garage, a storage building, or bedroom, attic, or basement, we always recommend not imposing on them. Regardless of good intentions, because you may be away for several months, your and their lives can change. Simply, your stuff may suddenly need to be moved. The following are some suggestions that may help.

House… If you plan to keep your house, then you must find some way for someone to take care of it. Unfortunately…

A. That can be expensive (to hire it done).

B. It may be a hassle.

C. You cannot let a house sit empty as it will deteriorate.

D. Murphy's Law says that something will go wrong (water leak, frozen pipes, rodents, whatever).

I always suggest that you not depend on friends who may volunteer to watch over your house for you. The reality rarely matches the intentions regardless of the sincerity of the parties involved.

Some RVers work out an agreement with a family member to "house sit" long-term. One couple let their grandson house-sit for them. The grandson was attending a local college and it provided a good situation for all. The grandson did not pay rent but paid utilities, insurance on the house, exterminator, association dues, etc. The couple kept the utilities in their name and the grandson deposited a check for his monthly utility costs directly into their bank account (anyone can make a deposit into your account without having direct access to the account). They were sharing the cost of the satellite TV.

Unfortunately, after about one year, the grandson moved on, the couple had to make the trip back to their house, and it required some extensive "clean up" to get it back to their definition of "normal."

Furniture… If your grand plan is to sell your house and when you are finished fulltiming, purchase another place (condo, apartment, house, castle, whatever), your existing furniture will likely not fit the new place either for style, color, size, or number of pieces. Sorry! Selling or having family members take custody of your existing furniture may be the best and easiest solution. Plus, if you do purchase another place sometime in the future, you will have some fun buying the new furniture for the new place. Having family members take custody may be a method for you to easily help them using familiar items.

Car… You will likely need a car to take with you unless you tow a 5th wheel or travel trailer. Then, of course, you must have a truck or other tow vehicle. We are a typical two-car-per-family nation. You cannot let your extra car just sit unless you specifically arrange for it. Car storage, like RV storage, is possible but you have to do certain things to get it ready to store.

There is the possibility of selling the extra car. One couple sold theirs with the plan to buy another car when needed. They ended up continuing to fulltime longer than they originally planned and were able to put off the new purchase for several years. A secondary result of this is cost savings.

There is also the car rental option. It is common for fulltimers with a drivable RV to sell all their vehicles and rent a car/4WD/truck when they really need one. The theory is that you don't need a car every day especially if you are located in an area with mass transit. Overall, your car rental costs will be significantly less than the cost of owning one. This approach is very common when traveling in a Class C or smaller Class A coach. However, very little fulltiming takes place in a Class C motorhome.

Family (Sentimental) Stuff... Selling a house or moving to a smaller place does not mean giving up your personal family "things." From old photos to antiques passed down through generations to mementos (non-antique sentimental items), these are important to most of us, give peace of mind, and allow us to reminisce with fond memories of good times long past.

These items should be stored in a controlled-climate storage. You can also ask a family member if they will store some for you. Again, this may not work if you have a room full of stuff to store. Our personal solution was that our two (grown) granddaughters and daughter took most of the items and the rest was stored.

How Do We...

The Rubber Hits the Road

Whether you reached this page by flipping through the book or reading from Page 1, this is the real deal. This is the concentrated "How To" stuff. The major chunks of information in here are the most common questions asked by people in our seminars, or e-mails, or during casual conversation in some RV park. We are regularly asked. We try to answer.

The information presented here is based on the concept of *"You are at home (in your RV) but your RV is not (at home)."* All those important functions we have to deal with on a daily basis when living in a house will also have to be dealt with on the road. While you won't have to mow the yard or paint a bedroom, you will have to continue banking, communicating (phone or mail) for business and pleasure, and deal with an occasional emergency. It is called "living" and it is what we do on a daily basis even though we planned something else!

How Do We Stay In Touch

We are often asked about no longer being able to see our friends or family on a regular basis or with the same frequency if you happened to be living close by. This will be a change for some, especially if your lifestyle is the type where you meet your friends once per week or month for some gathering. Perhaps you get together for a regular card game, potluck, or dinner out. Sorry, but that will go away.

On the plus side, when you do return and are able to visit, you will have lots of new things to talk about. An interesting note is that those same friends will, for the most part, think you are a little crazy, but will all be a bit envious of your new lifestyle. Perhaps your family will, too.

There are so many plusses! You will have ample opportunity to meet new friends. Gatherings of RVers are typically casual, often impromptu, and happen frequently. Simply, you can sit in your RV or join the crowd. Rallies, especially, are opportunities for gatherings and meeting new friends. Your life will change.

Staying in contact with family, friends, and business contacts is pretty easy today with your ability to make a phone call from nearly anywhere to nearly anywhere. This was definitely not true during my early RVing days. Then, we would have to search for a phone booth and always "schedule" a day and time for a call back home to ensure someone would answer. That was so long ago there were no answering machines either!

A Personal Story... Remember when we used to "schedule" fake person-to-person calls to ourselves to trick the operator so we wouldn't be charged for a real long-distance call? If it wasn't a "real" call, we wouldn't have to pay long distance charges but our family would know we were okay! For example, I'd call from Yellowstone Park to my folks in Indiana and say, "Operator, I want to place a person-to-person call to Ron Jones." Ring, ring. Mom would answer, "Hello, Jones residence." Operator: "Person-to-person for Ron Jones." Mom would come back with, "Ron is not here, he's on a trip to Yellowstone, but he's supposed to call this morning." You had to love those operators—and moms, too.

A Laptop is a Must

Living in an RV guarantees you less space unless you live in the tiniest of efficiency apartments. Therefore, big items don't fit very well. Desktop computers are too big for RVs—they just are. Get a laptop. Problem solved.

Laptops are designed to be portable. Desktop systems are not. One unusual fact about carrying a computer in an RV is that while you are moving—especially driving down the highway—the computer is vibrating. Just like everything in the RV, this vibration is somewhat detrimental to the life of the hard drive. The hard drive is a tough but delicate mechanism designed to operate flawlessly for years. While I have no proof, I am convinced that this nearly constant but slight vibration caused by the natural movement of the RV shortens the life of the hard drive.

Additionally, since you are regularly moving (traveling), you do not have the luxury of permanent Internet connections like you would in a house. It is easy to set up a wireless network in your RV or you can move the laptop as needed to plug in, for example, to your printer. We do just that. We store our printer in one larger drawer in the bedroom. When we need to print something (occasionally), we just carry the laptop back to the bedroom, plug in the printer, and print as needed. It works.

Our printer is one of those small combination units that prints, scans, copies, and a few other things that are unimportant to us. To reduce paperwork and filing, we use the "scan" function to scan documents and store them on the computer. This works well. I've also found that various business and government entities who "required" us to sign a document and fax it would accept that same document via e-mail. So, we will print the document, sign it, scan it, and send it as an e-mail attachment. If the entity will accept a fax, they will nearly always accept the attached, e-mailed document.

I strongly recommend a small external hard drive for backup purposes. The hard drive in your computer will, at some point, fail —they cannot last forever. When they do fail, your data and all those travel pictures will likely be history.

I also recommend an online backup service with an excellent reputation. Called "Mozy," you can set up a free account to store 2Gb of data. You set it (not difficult) to automatically backup every night after you go to bed. If you need to store more, there is a small monthly cost. I use them and they saved me from a couple of disasters. <https://mozy.com/home>

Purchase an external hard drive and set up the software to automatically backup every night—in the middle of the night. It's an easy safeguard for all that data and pictures.

There are a number of free (and paid) sites on the Web where you can backup your data. That is, the files on your computer are automatically copied to a website and stored nightly—accessible anytime by you if needed. The computer connects with the website at a preset time (such as 2:00 AM) and uploads only those files that were changed since the previous backup. This makes the nightly backup go fast. There is a limit to the amount of free storage space on the Web. More is available for a monthly fee and that is usually reasonable. However, to use this service, you must be online. Unless you have an Internet dish, this may not be a feasible alternative for backing up your data.

Internet

The Internet is not a "method" of staying in touch (like e-mail), but the basis for getting your message out to others. Therefore, understanding the various ways you can access and use the Internet will help and may save lots of frustration.

There are four easy ways to access the Internet... a dial-up modem, WiFi (wireless), cell phone, and satellite dish. All four work just fine but are radically different in efficiency and speed.

Dial-Up Modem... The traditional modem is fading from existence. There was a phone-line jack and generally, the connections were free to use.

They were fine for checking e-mail, pretty slow for playing (or serious searching) on various websites, and nearly impossible if you have to download larger files (like video).

WiFi... Wireless "hotspots" continue to increase worldwide and maybe, at some point, everything will be wireless. It's a great and easy way to connect to the Internet. There are a large number of businesses that offer free wireless connections and many computers automatically lock on (we did say "easy").

Additionally, some government entities now offer free wireless. Certainly for RVers, several states now offer wireless connections at official Rest Areas and Visitor Centers—Texas is leading the way.

Free WiFi is growing in many RV parks. Others charge a daily or weekly rate to use the network. Understand the costs before signing on.

One questionable practice is that a campground will offer free WiFi but charge for the Internet connection —almost a play on words but still, an additional charge, nevertheless. So the question for the campground is, "Do you have free WiFi and free access to the Internet? Are there any charges or fees?"

Often, the WiFi does not adequately cover the entire campground so ask for a spot with good reception when checking in. If it's really important that you get good reception, you can always grab your computer and drive the car back to the potential campsite to check the WiFi before moving in with your RV.

Even with a site located, it may be a sporadic connection. I typically work sitting at our dining table and I have had to move my computer to the dash in our motorhome to send/receive messages when connected through the local (campground) WiFi. Hey, whatever works.

Cell Phone... You may be able to use your cellular provider to connect to the Internet. This service is popular and the cellular connections are at least three times faster than dial-up modems. The first option is to connect your cell phone to your laptop (via either cable or Bluetooth). In this case, the cell phone acts as a "modem."

However, not all cell phones can be used for Internet access in this manner. Two things are required. First, you need some method to connect the cell phone to the laptop—a process called "tethering." Cellular companies typically don't sell cables for all their phones and a third-party cable may not work for Internet access. Second, the cellular providers do not routinely allow their phones to be used for Internet access without subscribing to a data plan of some sort, whether unlimited or by the kilobyte.

The second option is plugging a "data card"—sometimes incorrectly called an "air card"—or USB device into the laptop. Using this option, the data card or USB device acts as the modem. These devices are like cell phones with no voice service. These devices all require a data plan. Be sure to check for the monthly cost of the data plans and length of commitment. The devices may be discounted based on different plans.

Satellite Dish... A common solution is the satellite dish. One type of satellite dish can receive both TV and Internet 24/7. Generally, roof-top mounted on the RV, the dishes are automatic. Simply push a button to search and stow. A set-up-from-scratch, on-the-ground, tripod-mount dish is less expensive but more work—especially in a downpour.

With a clear shot at the southern sky, you can access both TV and the Internet in your RV while in the contiguous 48-states.

With those geosynchronous satellites permanently positioned over the equator, the farther south you go (think Key West here), the more the dish points straight up in the sky. The farther north you go (think Fairbanks here), the more the dish is aimed parallel or even pointing slightly down toward the ground. Therefore, at some point north, you will lose signal because of the curvature of the earth because it keeps trying to point to some satellite over the equator. My personal experience was that signals were still good as far north as Nova Scotia, Canada. I no longer own that system and cannot speak for connections farther north than Nova Scotia (about 46° North latitude).

Cell Phone

The nationwide coverage for cell phones today is okay but not perfect. You must be aware that there are a number of places all over the nation where cell phone coverage ranges from miserable to non-existent. There are estimates that only 50% of the USA is capable of cell phone service.

Most of these areas are out west but (my guess) there are some of these non-coverage areas in every state. Plus, phone companies simply have different coverage areas. Know that when traveling around the USA and Canada, you will be without cell coverage on occasion. There will be no warning—just no service. If you depend on your cell phone for connection to the Internet, you will, of course, lose this capability, too.

If you find yourself with no service, one "trick" is, to check for service as you approach any town or city. Again, especially out west, if you find service approaching a town, be sure to keep the conversation short as you will likely lose the service shortly after leaving the same town. The second trick is to power off the phone and restart it to ensure it locks onto an active cell tower if one is available.

Using your cell phone while traveling in other countries will cost you an international calling rate—this can be expensive. Some cell phone companies have a temporary international "calling plan" that is available for a reasonable monthly charge—or sometimes free—and is commonly available for Canada. This special plan will give you a reduced calling rate or possibly free calls depending on the service plan. You must ask your cell provider for details about this.

Special Numbers... Below is a list of suggested numbers that should be programmed into your cell phone before any major trip. Also, when saving these, or any numbers for use in your cell phone, save the numbers to the "SIM" card—that small storage card inside the phone. Ask your cell phone provider to show you how or read your manual—the information is in there. Saving numbers in this manner will allow you to easily transfer all your phone numbers to the next cell phone and save you reprogramming—a boring and tedious task. You just move the SIM card to the next phone and your programmed numbers are there, ready to use.

There are several other numbers that should be programmed into your cell phone especially when traveling for extended periods. It's easy to program them in, they are difficult to file or store in an RV, and you will want them handy.

- Your credit card Customer Assistance Phone Numbers (Not your credit card number)
- Insurance company (Car/Truck and RV)
- Emergency Road Service
- Emergency Medical Evacuation Insurance
- Doctors
- Bank
- RV Tech Support (Mfg.), dealer, or both
- Family and friends, of course.

A special word about "ICE" numbers... ICE (In Case of Emergency) numbers are used by law enforcement and emergency medical personnel IF you are incapacitated in any emergency. Most of us carry a cell phone. **Program your ICE numbers into your phone. Put the letters ICE first so it will show up on your phone number list.** You can easily designate multiple ICE numbers in several ways such as...

ICE - Wife - Kathy

ICE - Wife Work

ICE - Wife Cell

ICE - Daughter - Amy

Your ICE number should put the caller in contact with a person who is familiar with your medical condition and who may be able to speak with some authority on your care.

Regular Mail

It's nearly impossible to eliminate all that "regular" mail (often called "snail mail") but there are easy ways to manage it when traveling. I recommend stopping catalogs and junk mail plus cull through the magazines as you will have to pay for all the mail to be forwarded to you. Start this process several months in advance of that first extended trip.

The original sender pays for the mail to go to your mailing address. You must pay again to have it sent from your mailing address to where you are actually going to be. A mail-forwarding service will do that for you. FMCA (800-448-1212), Escapees RV Club (888-757-2582), and Good Sam Mail Service (888-726-6245) all have mail-forwarding services. Call all of them and compare services and prices.

A mail-forwarding service provides you with an address. Sometimes, as required by U.S. Post Office rules, that address will contain the designation for a "Private Mail Box" or "PMB." Your mail-forwarding address could look something like this...

> John Doe
> PMB 1234
> 5678 Main Street
> Anywhere, TX 12345-6789

The latest information states that the U.S. Post Office allows for the "#" to be used in the place of the PMB designation. Thus, your address could look something like this...

> John Doe
> 5678 Main Street #1234
> Anywhere, TX 12345-6789

Thus, your "Box" designation now looks like an apartment number. Regardless, the policies and rules can change at any time. You will need to check with your local post office to get the current status. I recommend you make the trip and talk to someone in person rather than calling.

The big advantage is that having this type of address provides you with a physical address and not just a P.O. Box. A physical address is required for the delivery of packages by the other services such as UPS, FedEx, and DHL—they will not deliver to a P.O. Box.

Note that when using a mail-forwarding service, your mailing address may be in a different state than your domicile (legal address). That is perfectly legal. Your domicile is the address you used when you are registered to vote and should be the address on your driver's license.

Our mail-forwarding service is our daughter. Our domicile (legal address) is different than our mailing address. The mail accumulates and she sends it to us when we can provide her with a local address where we will be.

We often use UPS Stores around the USA to receive our mail package but their "rules" change from store to store. Some will receive mail in your name, some won't, some charge, some don't. Don't assume it's okay and don't just assume a package can be sent without asking! You must call the store and ask if it is okay. We have also used a number of other shipping outlets and most charge a reasonable fee.

> *A Personal Story...* *I called one UPS Store and asked if I could have a package (my mail) sent to my name at their address (my usual question). The manager was emphatic, "No!," he said, "You could be receiving drugs!" So I asked if I could send a package from his store. He said of course I could. I then said that what I was hearing him say was that it was okay to send drugs through him, but not receive them!*
>
> *No, I don't do drugs. I was just being sarcastic. I thought his rules and reasons were pretty silly.*

Also ask the RV park if they will receive your packages while you are staying with them. This may easily solve your delivery problems.

I have used the USPS General Delivery twice and it worked fine. Two suggestions... Call the Post Office and ask for the exact address to use and use a small-town Post Office. We literally sort through our mail during a phone call with my daughter. Then she shreds junk mail. From my perspective, I believe if it's important enough to send, it's important enough to have a tracking number.

I do not recommend using the big UPS Customer Centers (those huge centers where they receive, sort, and put the packages on the trucks for local delivery) for receiving your packages. You can, but any incoming packages to be held for individual pick-up at these Centers must be labeled in a very specific manner, it's easy for them to miss, and you will be in a mess trying to locate your package. This happened to us once—but never again!

E-mail

Various providers offer free e-mail accounts. Setting up the account is easy and then, go to your provider's website, type in your user name and password, and you have access to send and receive e-mail. You can also send attachments such as documents or digital photos. Three common providers of free e-mail accounts are <**hotmail.com, yahoo.com,** and **gmail.com**>. There are others. Check carefully.

Blogs

A "blog" (combining the words "web" and "log") is a website where people provide personal commentary or news on a particular subject. People commonly use a blog as a personal, online diary or journal. Typical blogs combine text, images, and links. Links allow the reader to instantly and easily connect to other blogs, web pages, and other media related to its topic. Entries are displayed in chronological order. Blogs also allow readers to leave comments.

You can get free web space for your blog. One popular blog website is <**blogger.com**>. Owned by Google (a popular search engine), the blogging site works well and is easy to use for the novice. You can load text and photos of your trip and they will appear on a website for all to see. You furnish friends and family with the website address (URL) and they can call up your blog at their pleasure.

Blogs are nearly a perfect way to let family and friends know what and how you are doing—regardless of where you are traveling. You can post a daily (or less often) journal including your pictures and all of your family and friends can see/read it at their leisure. Your blog can be public—posted for anyone to see it—or private—only those you let in could see it. My blog can be found at

aboutrving.com/about_us.php##Blog

and is open to anyone to read. So, go ahead, take a look. Leave a comment, too.

While you could send the same information and pictures to anyone via e-mail, this would mean creating multiple messages every time—a lot of work and effort. Blogs allow the reader to also go back to an earlier time in the journey and review or catch up. Posting your blog today does not replace yesterday's posting.

VOIP (Calling via the Internet)

You can also use your computer and the Internet to make a phone call. The technical term is called VOIP (Voice Over Internet Protocol). You must download software (usually free) to your computer, log onto the Internet, and you can place a call to phones anywhere in the world.

You can use your computer's built-in microphone and speakers as your "phone." If the other party also has a computer and the software, you can have live video during the call—actually watch each other—if you both have cameras. It's great for staying in touch and seeing those little ones while you are on the road.

> *A Personal Story... When our great-grandson was 18 months old, we were concerned that he wouldn't recognize us since we were traveling 11 months. We used Skype (a VOIP) and our granddaughter would put Wesley in front of the monitor to see us when we called. Three years later, he still calls my wife, "Grandma on TV."*

How Do We Handle Finances

Dealing with money and banking while traveling requires you to approach handling your financial matters a bit differently. The Internet is an excellent source for accomplishing this. Is it perfectly safe? No—but no other method is either. I believe it is safer to access your accounts online as opposed to the traditional method of mailing general information, checks, statements, and personal information through normal mail.

Banks and financial companies have teams of people working diligently to ensure that your money, financial dealings, and personal data are safe. Think about it... keeping all that money safe is their business. Conversely, having mail (paper statements, checks, etc.) passing through numerous hands and then sitting in your mailbox is not something they can help protect.

We recommend that you also track your costs. After all, it's great to know what this lifestyle is really costing you. Tracking costs is very easy with a simple spreadsheet. As a side benefit, by watching your costs regularly, you will more likely know if or when someone happens to be "messing" with your account—identity theft is not a good thing.

With the Internet, you can view the status of your bank account, credit cards, investments, and other financial and personal information as much and as often as you want. In this age of "identity theft," I check my bank account and credit card statements daily. You have up-to-the-minute information rather than waiting for a monthly statement to be mailed.

When RVers use a mailing service, at any time financial documents are mailed to you in the traditional manner, the potential for problems expands. Your mail would leave the original sender, go to the mailing service, and then to you. This is like traveling from New York to Chicago by going through Miami! It does force your mail to pass through different places and more hands than if it were mailed directly to you (from Point A to Point B). Note this is not meant as any negativism toward mailing services. They do a great job and are necessary for your lifestyle.

Write No Checks

Most of us were raised to believe that paying by check is the ultimate method since there is a permanent record of the transaction—i.e., the cancelled check is proof of payment. However, we no longer write traditional checks unless we are absolutely forced to pay in that manner. Why? Again, based on the potential of identify theft, handing or mailing one of your personal checks to a total stranger is simply placing your personal data at greater risk. Think about this... When you send/hand someone your personal check, you are giving them most/all of the following information:

- Full name (often including middle initial and sometimes a title, e.g., Dr.)
- Address
- Home Phone, Fax Number, and Cell Number
- Driver's License Number

- Checking Account Number
- Bank's Routing Number
- Your Signature

With this specific and personal information, it is easy for unscrupulous people to steal from you. Interestingly, if someone suggested that you hand out this same information randomly to strangers, you would likely think they were somewhat crazy! Yet, you hand out this same information with every personal check you send or hand to strangers.

Banking

The ability to bank and pay bills on the Internet is wonderful. After 9/11, banks radically changed the way they do business and if you do not have an account with a bank, they will not do anything for you—not even make change. This negatively affected everyone that travels.

For fulltime RVers, the logical answer is a bank with the most "manned" locations in those areas where you plan to travel. We chose Bank of America because they are in the most states and so far, have been happy with our choice. I especially like their online banking. The site is easy to use, efficient, and seems to be up (working) all the time. I use the site at all hours of the day and, over time, have consistently found that their website is ready and working. I like and appreciate that.

Any incoming fixed monthly payments are direct deposited. This often provides me the money prior to when I would have received any check traditionally mailed. Any incoming random checks payable to us are sent to our mailing address (daughter). If she can determine that it is a check, she will open the envelope and let us know the amount and from whom. We may tell her to deposit it directly (anyone can make a deposit without having access to the account). We left a book of deposit slips for her to use as this makes the deposit process more efficient and less prone to error. This process has worked well for several years and we have no plans to change it.

For checks we may receive (this is rare), if we are traveling where we have bank access (a real bank), we deposit it. If we have no bank access, we send it to our daughter so she can deposit it. We do not use ATM machines, for any reason, period, and haven't used one since they were first available years ago.

Check with your bank and request they stop sending bank statements by traditional mail. Most will send you e-mail notification that your statement is available online. You can look at it or download and print it at your discretion.

The Safety of Your Personal Data

We frequently hear that people refuse to bank online because of the security issues. Your personal data (SSN, address, date of birth, etc.) is already in the bank's system whether you bank online or not. You were required to give them your personal data and it was input into the bank's system when you opened the account. When you pay bills or check your account online, you do not have to put your personal data in again (remember, it's already in there). You will have to log into their website and that will require a username and password.

After you have already logged into a website the first time, if, in the future, what appears to be that website asks for any personal data, that should be a red flag that someone may be attempting a scam or illegal operation.

The easy rule for you to follow is that if you ever get an e-mail or phone call *asking* you to log in to your account—it's likely a fake. Call your bank (or whatever company your account is with) and ask if the request is legitimate.

Paying Bills Online

Paying bills using online banking is efficient, easy, and safe. Paying bills will, of course, require that you put in the name of the payee and their address. Then, depending on the bank, a check will be sent (physically mailed) directly from the bank or funds electronically transferred to the payee (a bank-to-bank transfer). Either way, the bill is paid. Two things happen during the bill-paying process...

A. When you click to submit the payment, you are given a confirmation number that is valid for proof of payment.

B. You are typically given a choice of delivery dates for the payment. Being able to select the actual delivery date means that the bank will guarantee the bill will be paid by the date you select—a significant advantage to ensure you are never late with a payment. I set my delivery dates to be received (guaranteed by the bank) one business day before it is actually due.

The other good news is that paying bills through online banking automatically eliminates some of the information normally found on your personal checks. The checks sent directly from the bank usually contain your name, date, amount, payee, checking account number, and routing number. However, this is the minimum data required for any check and your personal address, phone, and other stuff typically printed on personal checks is not included. Less of your personal information is actually sent with the payment.

Your account balance is always current online. You can check daily or multiple times per day. When you make a deposit, you should be able to see it posted to your account instantly. This is radically different and far more efficient than waiting for that paper statement to be mailed out once per month. Banks still continue to issue that traditional monthly statement. As previously stated, they will mail it to you or you can access it online.

> *A Personal Story… It was coincidental that I was online, in our RV, in a parking lot, next to one of my bank branches. I went in, made a deposit, and walked back to the coach in less than a couple of minutes. Curious, I logged on to my account to see how long it would take for the deposit to show up. It was already there!*

One of the biggest negative banking functions is the unsolicited credit-card offers. For a fulltimer, having traditional mail catch up to you is one problem to solve but to pay the extra postage for mail forwarding on these offers is certainly irritating. Additionally, even having these "pre-approved" offers passed around enhances the opportunity for them to fall into the wrong hands. Try this…

> Call 888-567-8688 to opt out of the unsolicited credit card offers. This service is supported by the consumer credit reporting industry. Hey, whatever helps. We called and the sheer number of unsolicited credit card offers went down dramatically—not instantly, but over about a two-three month period. Regardless, something worked!

Credit Cards

I am a strong believer in using credit cards because of the itemized billing statements—I easily track my purchases and can check the status of my account online at anytime. The statements also make tax time and bookkeeping easier and far more efficient. I can store and easily access older statements if needed.

I am an equally strong believer in that you pay off your credit cards every month—no excuses—just do it. If you cannot do it, then you are spending too much for your income.

Credit Cards—Yes, for Traveling

Let's start with an assumption … Fulltime or not, when traveling, RVers are constantly in new areas and therefore, have no idea as to the safety potential or crime rate where you are located right now. Always think "safety." So I recommend you carry only two credit cards—note that the type of cards you carry is your choice. My focus here is on the number of cards.

I have three active credit cards but consistently only use one of them. I only carry two with me regardless of where I am traveling. Here is what we have and use…

- One VISA is a "cash rewards" card. It currently rebates 5% of all diesel and gas purchases, 2% of grocery purchases, and 1.25% for all other purchases. My rebate is itemized on the statement and deducted from the monthly bill. I use this card for all purchases if possible.

- One American Express (AMEX) for travel overseas (about once per year). In my experience, AMEX is nearly always accepted regardless of what some TV commercials are saying. They promote unlimited spending but at one time the "limit" was two times your highest monthly bill from the previous 13 months. However, a phone call could clear that limit if you needed to make a very large purchase.

- One VISA came with our checking account. We only carry this card when we need "account identification"—i.e., when we physically go into any Bank of America branch (our bank). I hand it to the teller and we are instantly identified as a customer—great for people like us who rarely go into the same branch twice.

The best reason for carrying only two cards is that the card data are easy to report if they should be lost or stolen. With that, keep the credit card numbers and the respective credit-card-company-customer-assistance phone numbers written down.

Store your "obvious" credit-card numbers in a well-hidden, safe place. Your wallet is not a safe place. Your purse is not a safe place. If you were robbed, your cards and your data would both be gone. Don't leave the data in your car as that could easily be stolen, too.

However, do program your credit-card company's customer-assistance **phone number** into your cell phone. There is a way to hide your credit-card numbers in your cell phone. In an emergency, you have it handy. Try this...

- AMEX uses 15 numbers. Hide your credit-card number by putting two fake phone numbers in your address book. It could look like this...

    Steve Johnson cell 999-9999

    Steve Johnson work 333-3333 x3

Note that **you have not used any area codes** so no one can try a random phone call to check on the validity of the numbers.

- Use this same technique for hiding your credit card numbers for any cards using 16 numbers (common with VISA). It could look like this…

Amy Brown cell   777-7777

Amy Brown work 444-4444 x44

If you should try this technique, I also recommend you add a few additional fake names and numbers throughout your address book. These should also look like the "Steve and Amy" entries suggested above. Think about it. The extra fake names can't hurt—after all, you know they are fake—and doing this may just help confuse the perpetrator if your data is stolen.

Check with your credit card company and request they stop sending monthly statements by mail. Most will send your statements via e-mail. It can't hurt to ask if they will also stop sending unsolicited offers.

If using a credit card online makes you nervous, one fulltime couple we know has another, totally different credit card they use just for online purchases. This particular card has a low maximum on it so if the card number is stolen, only a small number of purchases could be made.

Debit Cards—No, Never

I do not have or use debit cards. There are several reasons for this including…

- When you use a debit card, money is taken from your account instantly, i.e, it's like using cash without handling money. Give them cash instead of your card.

- It is estimated that over half of all overdrafts (spending more than what is in your account) were due to debit-card use. This means that the

$15.00 pizza could have cost you $50.00± because the bank allowed the debit-card charge to process even though you don't have enough money in your account! (Yes, I realize this sounds nuts but it's true. This practice was (hopefully) stopped with legislation in 2010.)

- When you use a debit card, excess funds in your account are often instantly "blocked." Called a "debit card hold," it is used by various agencies (travel, gas stations, car rental, etc.) to "block" or "hold" additional money to ensure you pay your bill in full. For example, if your car takes $35.00 to fill, a "hold" could be placed for $75.00 until the final bill is reported. Then, the difference ($40.00 in my example) is put back in to your account.

  The really bad news... the hold could stay on for several days! If you purchase gas on a Friday evening, the hold could last until Monday. An active hold means you have less money in your account thus automatically increasing the potential for an overdraft situation for many accounts. Note... If you have and use a PIN (pin number), doing so should eliminate the hold.

- Debit cards do not have the same protection against fraud as credit cards. With credit cards, you are disputing an unpaid bill. With a debit card, you are trying to get your money returned.

- I believe in using their money, for free, even briefly. A credit card allows you to do that. A debit card does not.

- **Never** use your debit card if the card will be taken out of your sight—common in restaurants where the waitstaff takes your card and the bill away from your table to be processed.

  Debit cards are prime for running through "skimmers" (electronic devices to copy your card's account info and security codes). Another device is then used to clone your debit card and any thief can access all your money instantly.

Never, ever, obtain a "fee-based" credit card as these will likely break you financially. Fee-based cards literally add "fees"—such as processing fees, maintenance fees, management fees, set-up fees, etc.—by simply tacking on these extra charges to what you owe! For example, you could have a charge of, say, $50.00 and with fees, owe the credit card company several hundred dollars. This is just nuts!

Password Protection

Numerous websites will require you to have password protection (a personal password) to enter any online site where you may have some personal data or an account. This is obvious with banking and credit-card accounts but passwords will be required for many other "personal" sites that you will need or want to access. These commonly include your e-mail, insurance, retirement, prescriptions, investments, your phone company, and virtually all your other "accounts," to name a few. Passwords are commonly required and regularly used.

Choosing a password is often an exercise in poor judgement, i.e., you choose an easy-to-remember password because, well, it's easy to remember! If it's easy for you, it's easy for anyone to guess it especially if they have just a bit of personal information about you. Since it's easy to find that information, it's typically easy to guess "easy" passwords. So, don't make it about you!

Here's just one way to choose a more unique password that is more difficult to guess. Take any two totally unforgettable (to you) but unrelated things and combine them to form your password. You need to have at least eight characters (some letters, some numbers) because some sites require that as minimum, but no symbols such as, but not limited to: @#)$&*+}%^ and no spaces (occasionally, symbols are allowed). Also keep in mind that some passwords on protected sites are usually case-sensitive. That is, there is a difference between a "B" and a "b" when used in a password.

There are methods for creating a password—customized just for you—that is also easy to recall. However, since you never, ever write down your passwords—anywhere—you must be able to literally figure out your custom password if you can't recall it at the moment. Here's one example for choosing an easy-for-you-to-remember password… use the city and state where your mother was born and combine it with your father's birth date. (Assuming you do remember this information and don't have to look it up.) Don't worry about capitalization so it could look like this…

> Your mother was born in Dallas, Texas so use the three letters: DTX (city initial and state abbreviation).
>
> Your father was born on: August 26, 1932 (08/26/32) so you will use 082632.
>
> They can be combined in various ways to form numerous passwords:
>
> DTX082632   082DTX632
>
> 082632DTX   D0T8X2632   and on and on…
>
> However, you only need one of these combinations.

Just remember, this is not about you so don't use your ZIP code, initials, phone number, home/work address, dog's name, birth date, SSN, license plate number, or anything else connected directly to you including your spouse's initials, phone number, work address, cat's name, birth date, SSN, or license plate number. Also, don't use something that may readily change such as an address.

Use two seemingly unrelated things that are very familiar to you. However, **use something you can easily recall** (or work it out mentally).

It works. It's not a perfect system. You can create a password that cannot be easily guessed by anyone even if they have limited information about you. However, don't write it down and don't send it to anyone.

Tracking Finances

If you have a business associated with your RV travel—as many do—then you must handle your accounting needs (tracking income and expenses) in some manner. The simplest method is by using a basic spreadsheet. This is what we do for our RV book and seminar business under our company name of "RV Stuff." Our spreadsheet tracks our income and expenses that we use for tax preparation.

Even if you do not have a business, I recommend you track your personal RVing expenses. You will be able to look back and make decisions based on former costs. It is easy to do and good information to know.

A simple spreadsheet works best. I recommend you put dates down the first column. Here are some suggested column headings you might want to use but, of course, customize it to fit your lifestyle.

Description… Explain it so you can recall a few years from now if needed while sitting in an IRS audit

Campground… What you paid including taxes, if any

Fuel… For the RV only

Transport… Major toll roads and ferry crossings

Maintenance… For the RV only

Tours and Tickets… We tour lots of places from the Shuttle Launch to tiny museums—it is a real cost.

Supplies… Not food or daily living supplies. We use this primarily for propane costs. If you stay at a campground where electricity is extra, note this in your description and put that electric cost in this column. Include supplies for actually running the business operation.

Fees… RV organizations, clubs, and rally costs

Miscellaneous… The classic catch-all column

Meals… A good idea if you eat out a lot. Breakfast, lunch, dinner, and snacks in separate columns. Our "meal" column shows a total cost of the meals for one day. We do not put groceries here—just eating out.

RV Mileage… Nice to know

Car Mileage… Nice to know, miles driven, not towed

The spreadsheet is easy to maintain daily and then, update it once per month when you download the statements from credit cards and the bank.

Our spreadsheet has every day of the year on it since we fulltime. After all, our coach is parked somewhere every night. I recommend you track the nights you boondock with a simple description such as *"Boondock, Wal-Mart, Abilene, TX"* or *"Boondock, I-10 rest area, mm 265, TX"* because doing this will help you recall the trip and daily progress. It will also ensure that you do not miss recording any nights since you either boondock, pay for a campground, or something else (the RV is always parked somewhere). For example, suppose your RV was in a service bay overnight and you had to stay in a motel. I would enter the motel costs in the Misc. column with a good description of where the RV was parked and why you were not staying in it.

How Do We Protect Ourselves and Our Stuff

I am a believer in security and protection for myself, my family, and my possessions. I am also a believer in doing it legally. There is lots of speculation and discussion as to the legal "status" of the RV—is it a vehicle (after all, you do drive it) or is it a residence (after all, you do live in it) or what is it? That answer is defined by state law (or provincial law in Canada) wherever you are at that particular moment. Just as speed limits change, so do laws concerning security and protection. Therefore, common sense goes a long way in keeping you safe and within the law.

> **It must be strongly noted here that both our international neighbors north and south—Canada and Mexico—have NO TOLERANCE for weapons crossing their borders. Don't do it!**

Weapons

We are frequently asked if we carry weapons in our RV. The answer is no, we do not currently carry any firearms. The reason is that we have crossed into Canada at least once per year for the last several years. You cannot take weapons into their country—legally. I highly recommend you not try it illegally. They and their dogs are very good at searching vehicles. I know this from experience.

If, in the future, we were **not** going into Canada or Mexico for a few years, I would again carry a firearm in our coach. I grew up with firearms, feel absolutely comfortable around them, know how to safely handle them, and should the need arise, would not hesitate to protect myself with them. This RV is my home—I have no other.

Having said that, if I were to carry again, I would do so legally like I did before. When we lived in Texas, we both took the classroom instruction and written test, qualified on the range, and for several years were licensed to carry concealed weapons. A number of states have reciprocal agreements and if you are licensed in one state, other states **may** acknowledge that agreement. Don't assume anything here, but check.

A Personal Story... One border crossing into Canada started with lots of questions from the booth person. I was told to pull over and go inside where they spent another 15 minutes going over the same stuff. We then waited while he checked both our driver's licenses (this was pre-passport days). We had a clean check. Then, at yet another counter, a fellow said he would like to take a look inside the coach. No problem. We walked.

There were three more Canadian custom's people waiting by our door. I went with the one outside and she went through every storage compartment —accessing both sides—and then our tow car, thoroughly. We went in our coach and one more agent had joined the group. They looked in every door, drawer, nook, and cranny—took their time —flashlights shining in the rear of those storage areas, carefully moving (a bit) things in front to be able to see in back.

Finally, one took me outside and asked if I had any weapons on board. I said no (the truth) and he said that he was getting his dog and that if there were any weapons or drugs, the dog would find them, period, the dog doesn't fail. I told him to get the dog.

Then the surprise—they had found two empty handgun "holsters" in the bedroom and again, did I have any weapons on board? No, I said that I had owned a handgun but sold it because we were going into Canada and that I had the receipt. He asked to see it. While looking at it, he attempted to ask some "tricky" questions—I guess trying to get me to say that I had a weapon. I didn't.

He got the dog (even carried it to the coach so it wouldn't walk through the water and mud outside). The dog went everywhere inside and we evidently got a clean "sniff." They never put the slides out and in the bedroom, crawled around on the bed to check everything. They even had the dog on the bed to allow it to check the rear closet.

After about 90 minutes of four people searching our coach, we were sent on our way.

There are numerous weapons including stun guns, tasers, batons, and various pepper and other types of spray to name a few. Many/most of these are illegal to take into Canada and Mexico. I strongly recommend that if you decide to cross their respective borders, do your research to find out what you can do legally. You always use the definition of "weapons" as defined by the country **you are entering**.

Interestingly, we regularly talk with people during our seminars who tell us they have no plans to go to Canada. That's fine (you will miss some outstanding country). Often, we ask for a show of hands for those planning to go to Alaska and many of those same people put their hand up. Think about it... to get to Alaska, you have to drive up through western Canada and turn left. The only way to get to Alaska and not cross the international border is via the ferry—an expensive option—but a great trip.

Securing Stuff

You may need to hide stuff in the RV. Some RVers take large amounts of cash with them, some take jewelry that they only wear occasionally, and you may have something special that is of value to you. You want it with you but do not need to access it daily.

One option is that you can purchase a safe to fit in an RV. If you choose to purchase one, I recommend a fireproof model. Also, if the safe can be welded into some part of the frame (such as a bed mechanism) from inside the coach, this may prevent it from "walking off" if a theft should occur.

Hiding Valuables

The good news is there are probably more good relatively accessible hiding places inside a large RV than there are in a house. The simple reason for this is that RVs are built with lots of hidden access panels throughout. These panels are found at the inside bottom or tops of cabinets, sometimes they appear as a normal part of a wall, or even in the ceiling. Access panels may be held in place by screws (sometimes bolts), Velcro®, spring-loaded drawer latches, or some other method. Often the screw heads or fasteners holding on the panel are hidden in fabric of some kind.

Removing one of the panels gives you access to some cavity. The RV manufacturer/designer uses these cavities for wiring, plumbing, and structural access—important stuff but hidden with the panel in place. The higher quality the RV, the better hidden (more nearly invisible) the panels are. When you take your RV in for service, if needed, the technician may need access through various panels. Also, when you talk to a technician, they can tell you where and how to access the various panels.

For someone not familiar with RVs—let's assume our potential "thief" is not an RVer—it is impossible to easily find these panels. The really good news is that even if our "thief" is an experienced RVer, different RV manufacturers put their access panels in different places and even secure them differently (screws, Velcro®, tape). Simply, stuff well hidden in an RV is going to be extremely difficult to find without taking the coach apart—not tearing it apart by simply going through and tossing stuff out of the cabinets but methodically using tools and dismantling it.

Hiding Cash

Note that anything hidden in this manner—behind access panels—will not be readily accessible. If you have to remove screws to access your hidden cash, you will not be able to do this in an emergency. In an accident, you may be able to return and access your hidden compartment. In case of a fire, you will likely lose whatever was hidden.

You must be creative in locating a hiding place you can use. In your underwear drawer or in an empty coffee can on your pantry shelf is not creative. This is too similar to a house. Find someplace in that RV that is unlike any part of a house.

Ditch Bag

For the non-boaters reading this, a "ditch bag" is a waterproof, buoyant bag that contains items critical to your survival if your boat sinks. The boater's ditch bag usually has various items related to food, water, shelter, and communication. It's small, easy to grab when going over the side or sinking, light enough to easily handle, and contains absolutely essential items. **It's what you are left with when everything else is gone.**

You may want to consider carrying a "ditch bag" in your RV. Lots of RVers do. Granted, your RV is not likely to sink but disasters can happen. One of the worst is fire. A fire will consume an RV rapidly—in a few minutes. Regardless of what you think you can do or take out of the RV, consistently, RVers who have actually gone through a fire have stated there is barely enough time for you to get out.

For RVers, putting together a ditch bag is common sense. You make it easy to grab on your way out of the coach in an emergency. It sits by the door in the daytime and in the bedroom at night (in case you have to go out the emergency escape windows).

What do you put in a ditch bag? As with other lists, my list will likely not work for you so I won't offer it. However, you may want to consider things such as copies of your insurance policies, a copy of your driver's license, list of emergency phone numbers, some cash, extra set of keys for the truck/car, an LED flashlight (the tiny ones are great), a couple of the cheap plastic ponchos, a throw-away cell phone, and (if you spend time way off the road parked in BLM lands) maybe a signal mirror, bottle of water, power (energy) bars, and on and on. **It's what you want in hand when everything else is gone.**

[Note: A perfect signal mirror is a used CD. They have a mirrored surface and hole for sighting.]

Your ditch bag should be small enough that it is not a problem to grab on the way out of the RV. Plus, you should take this bag out of the RV every time you vacate it for some period of time—e.g., take your ditch bag with you in your truck/car when you go to the grocery. Put it back in the coach when you are staying in the coach whether parked or driving. The ditch bag stays with you.

Doing this means you are prepared for an emergency while you are out of the RV. Do not leave the ditch bag in your tow car while driving the RV. You want it with you—accessible. A hooked-up, towed vehicle will likely burn if there is an engine fire in a rear-engine motorhome. Therefore, your ditch bag needs to be where you have rapid access to grab it—not stored in another vehicle.

Extra Keys

I recommend hiding a full set of keys somewhere on the RV. This hidden set needs to be accessible outside since the assumption is that you are locked out of the RV for whatever reason. Your hidden set would include an ignition key, door key, compartment keys, among others—whatever you need. If you have a motorhome, don't hide anything in your tow car—it's easy to steal. The extra keys may not fit in one of those little magnetic boxes that you can buy everywhere. However, if you are going to go to the trouble to hide a set, then hide all the keys you might need.

Put this set of keys together in double (two) zip-close plastic bags, give the keys a squirt of silicon lubricant (like you use on your RV) to prevent any rust or pitting, wrap and squeeze the air out of the bag, seal it, and tape it shut. You can also use one of those "food saver" machines that create a vacuum in the bag. Using black, electrical tape (not duct tape because it is grey and easy to see), tape this lump of keys **on top of some part of the RV frame underneath the coach**. Tape it on top so it cannot be seen by just looking or even crawling underneath—you have to know exactly where it is to actually put hands on it.

Yes, if you ever have to get these keys, you may have to crawl in the rain or mud. But that's okay. Getting those keys is only done in an emergency and hopefully, it won't happen during the life of your RV. However, you do not want that lump of keys to be spotted accidentally by the person changing your oil, working under your coach, or anyone snooping around your coach when you are gone some night.

Common Sense

RVers frequently stay in geographical areas where they have no idea of the potential problems that exist locally. From crime rates to local unrest, people traveling can easily find themselves in the middle of  trouble. Common sense plays a large role in staying safe.

Here's a different way to think about it... *You are at home (in your RV) but your RV is not (at home).* Therefore, it's easy to become complacent about your surroundings.

I have a large motorhome. It looks fine. It is my home. It cost as much as a home. It is impressive to others. I am sure there are some people who think that because I have this very nice RV, I must have considerable wealth and carry it with me. I don't, but they don't know that.

We often boondock (dry camp) and, always with permission, do this at Wal-Mart, Flying J, Rest Areas, and numerous other places. We typically do not use a campground unless we need their services. Interestingly, we have been in some campgrounds that looked pretty "seedy"—i.e., while driving through, I really wasn't sure if I wanted to stay there. Regardless of where you stay, there are some precautions you can take to make yourself and your RV a bit more safe. Consider the following...

- Lock your doors and windows. Lock your compartments around the RV. Lock your tow car.

- If you have an electric step, put it in at night and lock it with the switch. Lock it so that it will not automatically go out if the door is opened.

- On a motorhome, if you have a step cover for the inside step well, put it out (over the well) at night. This creates somewhat of a barrier should the door be opened.

- When boondocking in a parking lot, park under a light with your door facing the front door of the store.

- Put your curtains down. Don't make it easy to see in.

- Don't leave your computer on the dash where it is visible to everyone.

- Don't leave your computer cables and wiring hanging out under the front curtain on the dash when parked overnight.

- Don't leave your GPS attached to the windshield and visible.

- Never open the door to a stranger. Answer any knock on the door by sliding open a kitchen or other window and talking from there.

- If it's the police, ask them to hold up their badge, get a badge number, and then ask them to point to the police car. Police rarely walk any more.

- Call the local police to see if it is really the police. If it is truly an emergency, dial 911.

- Program 1-800-466-4411 into your cell phone. This is a free combined US and Canadian business directory.

- If someone approaches your coach and asks for gas/food/shelter/car repair money or says their spouse is sick/their dog just got hurt/their child just fell, tell them you will be happy to call the police and ask them for any type of local charitable service that provides this sort of help.

- Many automatic satellite dishes have a built-in light shining on the dish and it looks like a beacon at night. Simply turn off the power to the controller inside. The light will go off but the dish should continue working. Turn the power to the controller back on to stow the dish.

- Use your rear camera monitor to see what is happening behind your RV.

- If you see or hear people messing with your tow car, hit the "Panic" button on your car's keyless clicker while standing inside your RV. If it won't signal the car through the rear of your coach, reach out the bedroom window to do this.

Let me close this section by stating that I have never had a single problem in any location, in any RV, anywhere. There have never been any break-ins nor an attempted break-in that I am aware of for any RV I have owned in the last 25 years. I have been approached on a few occasions by individuals who were asking for money for some reason (gas, groceries, fuel, doctor, etc.). However, I have been approached with the same question more often in gas stations and on the street than I have in the RV. My consistent response to this type of inquiry is that I would be happy to call the police and ask them for any type of local charitable service that provides this sort of help.

We do not seek out questionable locations or areas to park our coach— even if it is just for one overnight. We have called the state police and asked for information

about any potential or history of "problems" in particular rest areas. They were candid and I greatly appreciate that. We try to stop a few hours before dark. We can better judge the area in daylight and leave if we are uncomfortable.

The only incidents (but not problems) we have had was the rare but occasional vehicle or motorcycle driving by with the loud muffler or the radio blaring. Once or twice, we have had what we assumed to be high-school kids blowing their horn as they were driving by our parked coach. However, all of these incidents were rare, happening less than a handful of times during the hundreds of nights we have spent not in a campground.

How Do We Deal With An Emergency

Campground owners usually maintain lists of phone numbers in their office for numerous local emergency services. They regularly deal with RVers who know nothing about the area and, when needed, this is welcome information. You are an RVer and likely have a campground directory to find the campground phone number. Motels and hotels also keep emergency numbers as a service to their guests. They will share information with anyone in an emergency. Drive into the hotel/motel and ask in person.

Some RVers program the local police emergency phone number (not 911) into their cell phone when they are staying in an area for a while. But be aware that there are numerous places, especially in the west, where cell phones will not work at all. There is no service regardless of your carrier.

> **Dialing "911" on your cell phone...** This **should** connect you with local emergency services regardless of where you are located. For example, assume your cell phone is registered to a 940 area code (Denton, Texas) and you are traveling in Montana (406 area

code). Suppose you see an emergency in Montana and call "911." The local (Montana) cell tower that picks up the call signal **should** send the call to the **local** (Montana) 911 operator—not back to Denton, Texas.

A number of GPS programs contain searchable business data (including phone numbers). With some brands, you can purchase extra business and personal data (more listings). While it is handy for finding a local pizza place, it is great for finding medical help of nearly any kind. You must know how to search the program for the specific type of business so it is necessary to learn this process before actually needing to use it. For a true medical emergency, the GPS may be the least efficient method for locating help.

Medical Emergency

Medical problems happen and the longer you are on the road, the more likely it will happen to you. We have been lucky. Other than an occasional cold and one trip to an emergency room for a cut thumb, nothing major had ever happened—until this...

> *A Personal Story*... *We were in a totally strange area. We just pulled into New Bern, North Carolina, had a campground reserved, and were going to be a tourist there. It's what we do.*
>
> *Sandy was not feeling well (rare) but we went out for a quick dinner that first night. The next day, she was still feeling just fair. The third morning she said maybe she should see a doctor. You should note that when either one of us says that, we go— it's past time for discussion or home remedies.*
>
> *The campground told us about a walk-in medical clinic (20 minutes away) that took us right in, checked her, and suggested she go to the*

emergency room. We did. She checked in, they ran tests, and diagnosed appendicitis—about to rupture! Within a couple of hours, she was in surgery and a 45-minute procedure turned into a 2.5-hour major surgery due to the contamination. Two days later, she was home, we had an extended stay in that campground for another week, and she was pronounced fit to travel with minor restrictions.

The campground owners, medical staff, everyone, were totally helpful, professional, and caring for two total strangers literally passing through. We will always be grateful for that.

There was nothing we could have done to actively prepare for that experience. It was truly an emergency. We did, however, consider it a true "test" of our lifestyle and the test was positive. Everything, from the local people's reaction and help to the insurance claims, was handled efficiently. The fact that we traveled fulltime in our motorhome never entered the picture except to provide a few smiles, an occasional question, a few odd looks, and some lively conversation.

Prescriptions

Receiving your normal prescriptions does not constitute a medical emergency. However, prescriptions are "medical" and some may be life-threatening if you miss taking them. The good news is that today, getting your prescriptions filled while traveling is much easier than ever before. All major pharmacies and chain-stores with pharmacies are connected within their respective major networks. For example, CVS pharmacies are all connected, Walgreen's pharmacies are all connected, Wal-Mart pharmacies are all connected, as well as others—however, independent pharmacies are typically not. Your doctor can fax or call in a new prescription (or refill) to a local store **and ask that it be held until you call for it.** Then, wherever you are traveling (within the U.S.A.), you can call locally to that same brand of pharmacy nationwide, ask them to get it ready, and pick it up with a very short wait.

> **[Note: If you have a written prescription in hand, but your existing prescription is not yet due for a refill, you cannot get the second prescription of the same type filled—without special approval.]**

The scenario that causes this to happen is if you spill or lose your pills. For example, in your RV, suppose you accidentally spill all your pills into the sink—filled with dishwater. So, you locate a local pharmacy, then call back to your doctor and explain you need replacement pills, and provide the doctor with the pharmacy phone number. Next, the doctor calls in the prescription order to that pharmacy. When you show up to pick up your prescription, the pharmacy will block the order from being filled—because their records or your insurance will indicate that you already have pills. It's not time for another (overlapping) prescription!

You will have to get your insurance provider or prescription service to approve the new prescription. Only then will you receive your prescription. Note that this is not a question of who will pay but of overlapping prescriptions. Even though your doctor writes a new prescription, it does not automatically go through the system to be filled. Either the insurance will put a hold on the refill (due to overlapping prescriptions) or the pharmacy will stop it if you previously filled the prescription with any of their stores. This process is in place to prevent people from obtaining multiple prescriptions for controlled substances.

Another situation where you may run across overlapping prescriptions is when planning to travel extensively out of the USA.

For example, let's assume your current prescription is not yet due for a refill but you are getting ready to leave the USA for some extended trip. You will need more pills (an additional prescription) before you go since you don't have enough on hand to last until you return to the USA. However, it is not time for your refill. Let the pharmacist know about your trip before they attempt to fill your prescription. It may help them to expedite approval and ultimately make your life a bit easier.

[Note: Ask the pharmacy for coated pills. They won't get all powdery from vibrations in the RV.]

Dental Emergency

Fulltimers will at some point experience dental problems. Dental facilities seem to be more focused on long-range fixed appointments than medical clinics. You rarely see a walk-in dental clinic. However, you can get in for emergencies. Even so, it may take a day or two.

> *A Personal Story... We happen to be in Gilroy, California (the garlic capitol) one summer, having dinner, and I broke a tooth. I am a member of an e-mail group for Monaco owners so I posted a message asking if anyone had knowledge of a dentist near Gilroy.*
>
> *A fellow replied immediately and recommended a wonderful dentist in San Jose (about 40 miles from us). The next day I called, they got me right in, and that dentist did a temporary crown that lasted about six months—long enough for us to return to our regular dentist.*
>
> *Interestingly, I had the same experience (different tooth and city) the following year, too.*

Vehicle Emergency

There are two kinds of vehicle emergencies—one type with the RV and the other with your car. For RV emergencies, there are two types that are considered really bad—one is a fire in the RV and the other is being in an accident. We realize there are others, too. Depending on the severity of the accident, either emergency will instantly stop you from continuing your lifestyle. However, and especially if you are fulltiming, you can't just leave your RV behind and go on without it.

In case of an accident, you have to consider the security of your personal stuff in the RV if the RV is not livable and possibly cannot be secured (locked). If you go spend the night in a hotel room, how do you secure your stuff (again, if needed, depending on the severity of the accident)? While this cannot be answered here, it is something to occasionally think about and be aware of. Unexpected things happen.

An RV fire is usually a disaster due to several reasons...

- RVs are fast-burning and unless you were parked by the firehouse, the fire department would rarely be able to get to your location in time to save your stuff.

- You likely carry that dinky fire extinguisher mounted by the manufacturer next to the door in the RV. It may help in a very small fire.

- You probably have no "fire plan" for evacuation of the RV should something happen.

- You may not have time to unhook your other vehicle whether you are towing it or towing with it.

- If a fire occurs, you will likely be in a strange place.

Should a fire take place while you are in bed or your escape from the coach through the exit door is blocked. I recommend you carry an escape ladder in case you have to go out the emergency escape windows (the ones with the ugly red handles). Using these handles will cause the window to open fully and there is room for you to get out. That's the good news. The bad news is that it is a long way down to the ground, the trip will be short, fast, and have a sudden stop. Likely, it's going to hurt!

The answer... Think about an "escape ladder." These flexible, foldable ladders were originally designed for second-story bedrooms and apartments. They hang over the window sill and literally unroll down the side of the house, apartment building, or in our case, the RV—after you open the emergency escape window.

The ladders have a type of modified "grappling hook" and simply hang over the opened window. They are not permanently installed and roll or fold into a small "package" ideal in an RV. Store it next to the bed—not in one of the compartments underneath! The one shown here rolls up to about the size of a shoe box but will hold 1,000 pounds! You can spend less than $100.00 and sleep safer.

Some of the best RV fire information is available from Mac McCoy (aka "Mac the Fire Guy"). He specializes in educating RVers about RV fires. His website is and there, you can learn about RV fires, fire extinguisher maintenance and operation, and get those checklists, too. Also, attend his seminars at various rallies and shows. I guarantee you will learn things that may save you or someone's life.

You can certainly have an emergency or breakdown with your "toad" (tow car) or your truck (or other vehicle) used for towing your RV. Traditional vehicles—cars, trucks, SUVs, etc.—will need to be serviced regularly (grease and oil) and they occasionally break down. Among new RVers driving a motorhome and towing a vehicle, there is an occasional rumor that since the car's engine is not actually running while being towed, you can go longer without servicing it. Not so.

While it is true that the engine is not running, on some vehicles, "everything" underneath is moving—i.e., wheels are turning, axle, drive shaft, gears in the transmission, etc. are turning when the vehicle is being towed. Therefore, it is recommended that you continue to follow the manufacturer's mileage recommendation for servicing. The odometer on some vehicles will not work when towing—i.e., no miles are added. If this is the case with your tow vehicle, simply add the driving miles (from the vehicle's odometer) to the towed miles (from the RV's odometer) to determine when servicing should be scheduled.

Most vehicle dealers are connected online nationwide with warranty and repair information about your vehicle. We drove a Saturn Vue for four years and any time we stopped for service, dealers throughout the USA and Canada were all sharing information about our car.

Family Emergency "Back Home"

Sometimes, the "emergency" is with your family and due to your fulltiming lifestyle, your current location is not close by. You may also just need to make a quick non-emergency visit—we have returned for one wedding and one birth—thankfully at different times. You have three choices: public transportation, car, or return in the RV.

As a side note here, we have our two carry-on suitcases with us in the RV at all times. We do not carry any large suitcases with us. If we need the large ones, our daughter will ship them (empty) to wherever we are. Because we rarely use those carry-on bags, they are handy for storing long-term items—i.e., heavy winter coats, rarely worn boots, etc.

Public Transportation... A flight, train, or bus is your option. Lots of RVers use a credit card for expenses while RVing (fuel, campgrounds, eating out, etc.) and have the accumulated credit card "points" converted to frequent-flier miles. They use these miles for emergency tickets.

RVers can often take advantage of simply driving to a major airport and staying close by. Flight fares may be less from major airports than from some obscure location. Itineraries are nearly always more flexible. Smaller airports typically require additional flight segments—often in small aircraft.

We typically drive our RV to a campground (up to 100 miles from the airport), but then actually drive our personal vehicle to the airport. The combination works well. It provides security for the RV while we are gone, allows us to access major airports to reduce flight costs, and parking a normal car near an airport is easy to do.

Personal Vehicle... If you find an ideal location to leave your RV, you can drive your personal vehicle. While your family may provide a place to stay, having your own transportation available may be very helpful. Driving the personal vehicle will be less cost in fuel than driving the RV.

Drive the RV... Sometimes it is best to drive the RV to the "emergency." The obvious disadvantage is the length of time it takes—there simply may not be time to get to where you need to be. Cost is also a factor especially if you want or need to return to your existing location.

The obvious advantages are that you have your "home" with you, can live normally for any length of time, will not be intruding as a "house guest," have your own transportation (car or truck), and regardless of the length of stay, you will be prepared. While you may have to interrupt your planned trip, doing so will also create the opportunity for alternative destinations or routes.

Personal GPS Tracker

I have always been concerned that I might break down somewhere without cell service and no satellite (online access). In preparation for our trip to Alaska, my concern was growing. That trip proved there were many lonely miles where something could have happened. I was on one stretch of highway that had a sign warning drivers that it was 103 miles to the next services. Nothing happened and that's good. If something should happen, you simply wait for the next vehicle to come by.

In researching an alternative method of contact for emergencies, I found a product called the SPOT—a personal GPS tracker. The product is primarily sold and marketed to back-country hikers/backpackers. It's small (7 ounces) and you use it when you need it.

There are three message options on the SPOT. You set these up on a password-protected web page. The first two are your custom messages and mine are below. The 911 button is automatic.

- **Check In**... "I'm just checking in—everything is OK! Ron" (I send this from wherever we parked for the night.)

- **Ask for Help**... "Need HELP - likely broke down. Not bleeding so NO 911. No cell. No e-mail. Send help to coordinates. Ron/Sandy."

- **Alert 911**...Note: when you hit the 911 button, SPOT acquires its exact coordinates from the GPS network and sends that location plus a distress message to a GEOS International Emergency Response Center every five minutes until cancelled.

Whenever the "Check In" button is pushed, a brief e-mail goes to all recipients you have entered into the system. The recipient can click on the link in the e-mail and our exact location shows up on a Google map.

I'm glad we had it and we didn't use emergency services.

Emergency Road Service

One common type of special RV insurance is called "Emergency Road Service." It is designed to provide financial assistance, technicians, or professional help for minor emergencies while you are on a trip. I highly recommend this, have carried it on every RV, and have used it when needed. It is inexpensive—often less than $100.00 per year.

Emergency Road Service provides you with help for those common mishaps such as running out of fuel, towing, or flat-tire service. On a large motorhome, it would be extremely rare for anyone to have the tools on board to enable them to change a tire. It is also rare that you would even carry a spare. Therefore, the service is invaluable—especially for the cost. But, as always, read what you are paying for before you buy. Consider these commonly included services…

Flat-Tire Service… Qualified technicians are dispatched to change a tire and may include locating and delivering a new tire.

Towing to the nearest Service Professional… May pay 100% of RV towing fees to the nearest independent professional service center. Actual towing distance may be unlimited.

Emergency Fuel Delivery… Typically, 5 gallons of fuel will be delivered.

Lost Key & Lock Out Service… A pre-paid locksmith is dispatched to your location.

24/7 Toll-Free Emergency Dispatch… You can always reach a real person.

Roadside Repairs… A mobile mechanic is dispatched to make minor roadside repairs to your vehicle.

Protection For Household Vehicles… May include cars, pick-ups, SUVs, motorcycles, and even boat trailers.

Spouse & Children Protection… May include spouse and children under 25 years old living at home or attending college.

Emergency Medical Referral Service… Assistance with personal or medical emergencies related to an accident or illness while traveling.

Trip Interruption Help... Reimbursement for meals, rental car, and lodging if your vehicle is disabled due to a collision. Typically, you must be over 100 miles from home.

Emergency Medical Evacuation Insurance

The primary purpose of Emergency Medical Evacuation Insurance is to provide help during medical emergencies and to assist with travel arrangements after the situation is resolved. The insurance pays for an emergency evacuation when it is deemed medically necessary for the patient to obtain a higher level of care. The following (between the lines) was reproduced verbatim, with permission, from the FMCA website.

The FMCA contracted with MEDEX Assistance Corporation to provide active family and life members with coverage under the MEDEX PLUS Program. This program helps traveling members to effectively manage the complexities and expenses of out-of-area medical and travel emergencies. Members receive this coverage with no sign-up required.

MEDEX provides members with toll-free access to travel assistance services and also coordinates and pays the approved costs associated with the following:

- Emergency medical air and ground evacuation: Medically supervised evacuation to the nearest appropriate facility if an FMCA member is involved in an accident or suffers a sudden, unforeseen illness and adequate medical facilities are not available.

- Repatriation of remains: The return of an FMCA member's mortal remains in the event of death.

- Return home of unattended grandchildren and dependent children: Transportation home for an FMCA member's children and/or grandchildren left unattended as the result of a member's accident, illness, or death.

- RV and automobile return home: Return of an FMCA member's drivable vehicle to his or her residence (or return of a rental vehicle) if the member is unable to operate the vehicle due to accident, illness, or death.

- Transportation to join a hospitalized member (for member traveling alone—if member is hospitalized for seven days or more): The transportation of a family member or friend to visit an FMCA member who is hospitalized for seven days or more.

- Transportation home after initial evacuation: The transportation of an FMCA member to the point of origin, or permanent residence, following an emergency evacuation.

A variety of types of Emergency Medical Evacuation Insurance is offered/sold by a variety of companies—some are connected to the RV industry but some are not. As always with purchasing any insurance, you should carefully compare the benefits and costs before making a purchase. However, it must be noted that as of this writing, FMCA membership includes MEDEX Assistance Corporation's Emergency Medical Evacuation Insurance as part of normal dues and at no extra charge.

How Do We Know What to Take With Us

Regardless of how long you have been an RVer—especially a weekender—you will over-pack for that first extended trip. It just happens. Those dreaded "Well, we might need this" thoughts sort of prevail and it's just hard to leave some of that really useful, important stuff in storage when you drive away. This is pretty normal behavior.

The harsh reality is that you can't take everything you had in the house. But the good news is that you can take a lot of stuff. You just need to think a bit differently  about how to select what you will take. But first, you need to know how much you can take—legally—based on the size and configuration of your RV. Yes, there is a limit and it is based on your RV.

Now, if you need me to furnish some lengthy packing checklist for you that includes, for example, a flashlight, extra blank checks, towels, your insurance card, and toilet paper (to name just a few of the hundreds of items), then this would have to be a very long and boring chapter. The truth is, I have no idea what you will need personally. Make up your own list.

I think you will find it more efficient to think about groups of stuff—food, clothing, tools, entertainment, other. Quantity will be determined by the available storage in your RV. Both the size of the RV and the layout will mandate the total quantity of items you take with you.

Consider this... The stuff you need to live efficiently and comfortably in your RV is the same stuff you **used** in your house—but just **not as much of it**! For example, if you occasionally use flour in preparing one of your favorite recipes, then you will need flour in the RV. But instead of buying the 10-pound or 5-pound bag, consider the 2-pound or 1-pound bag. If you have a place setting for twelve, you will not need that in the RV. We take with us a place setting for six. If we had to provide table service for more than that (and I can't imagine when that could happen), we would provide the plastic utensils.

This same thinking also applies to the variety of foods including canned goods, packaged foods, spices, etc. For example, you may use sage (the spice) in several recipes—if so, pack it in the RV assuming it is not the gallon-size container you got on sale. I use chicken broth frequently in my cooking (yes, I cook). When we lived in our house, I would buy chicken broth in cartons, measure what I needed, and store the remainder in the fridge. Now, living in our motorhome, I still use chicken broth but buy it in the granule form. A very small jar will make a gallon of excellent broth, doesn't need to be stored in the fridge, and takes up only a small space in the pantry.

The worst offender for consuming space is clothing and shoes. If you had six closets in your house, you likely have six closets full of clothes and shoes. You didn't wear all of them during any particular season. Now, you can't take them all with you. How do you decide? First of all, one reasonably dressy outfit will suffice for most RVers. This is just not a "dress up" lifestyle.

Your clothing choice will be mandated by where you plan to go so first, select the type of clothing based on the climate and temperature. Now, choose what outfits you would wear for the next 14 days (no repeats but you should not need 14 changes of underwear). So, you ask, what do I take?

Your number of outfits is totally dependent on …

- Your storage space
- Your style of dress
- Where you are going. If you are headed from Dallas,Texas to Fairbanks, Alaska you have to pack both heavy and lightweight clothing.
- Your plans for doing laundry. A washer/dryer in the RV is extremely handy. There are laundromats in most cities and small towns plus many campgrounds will have some laundry facilities.

[Author Note: If you are driving your RV, small town laundromats often have larger parking areas than those in the city.]

You can change the magic number of "14" to whatever you want so long as your clothing will fit in the RV. However, starting with that number will provide you with a guideline for prioritizing your selection.

This thinking applies to everything you may want to take ranging from kitchen chairs to underwear to books. You used all this in your house and will need those same things in the RV—but just **not as much of it!** These kinds of decisions are important because they affect your overall RV weight (it's illegal to be overweight) and your physical living area (with something stuffed in every nook and cranny).

A Word About Packing Safety

It is easy to have everyday items sitting around in your RV. There is a natural tendency to do this, especially when parked for a few days. The coffee pot, toaster oven, dish drainer, etc. are commonly found on the counter top while framed pictures, boxes of tissues, computer, magazines, books, and maybe a potted plant are also sitting out. It is common to see, for example, a parked motorhome with stuffed toys sitting on the dash. What happens to these items when you leave—i.e., when you are driving your RV down the highway?

Many RVers will use the non-slip, rubber-like material on counters and surfaces to prevent these items from moving while the RV is being driven. However, this is **not safe. Items sitting on a counter top will literally turn into flying missiles in a sudden (panic) stop.** Getting hit from behind with a loaf of bread may be okay but getting hit with the coffee pot is not. You must pack and store items when traveling.

Personal Information

The longer you plan to fulltime (actually be on the road continuously), the more personal information you will need with you. The best example of this is if you are going to be traveling from January through April, you will need all your financial information from the previous year to be able to complete and file your income tax.

Much of this personal information is on paper so organizing and filing is an ongoing chore—just like living in a house. You will need a file drawer built into your RV (as many already have) or purchase one of those file boxes from an office supply store. Buy the smaller file box as you will have to store this box somewhere in the RV—typically underneath in a storage compartment. If so, make sure the compartment is waterproof. Even if you have lots of files and have to purchase a second one, two smaller boxes are easier to manipulate and store than one large box.

Many people now scan their documents into their computer and store this data online. The space saved is significant. This is fine but takes an organized person to do it conscientiously. Plus, what do you do with the original paperwork after scanning?

Long before actually driving away for that first extended trip, lay out (on the dining room table or a spare bed) those papers and documents you think you need to take with you in the RV (this may be most of your financial information from the last year). Get them organized (file folders). If you have never organized this before, you are going to have lots of hard work ahead of you to accomplish this.

Got what you need (or think you need)? Great. Now organize, label, and file the documents you are leaving behind so that if you need something, someone else can get it for you.

Clothes

With clothing, you have to know what kind of RV layout you have (or are going to purchase) and how you like to have your clothes arranged. By this, I mean some RVs have decent-to-large closets. For example, ours has an eight-foot-long, full-length, hanging space across the total rear of the motorhome. Closets are important to us—drawers are not.

Other RVs have almost no hanging space (by design) but have large drawers that will hold lots of folded clothing. If you like to hang your clothes, drawers are not recommended and vice versa. Remember the rule… you can take the same stuff you used in your house—but just not as much of it.

Take a look at where you plan to go (in general). It's easy to check the annual average weather in major locations. This gives you an idea of local temperatures at the approximate times you will be there, and you pack accordingly. The good news is that you do not have to be super-selective like if you were packing to stay at a hotel. For example, we do not plan to be in any snow so heavy winter clothing never goes with us.

Take a range of clothing. We each pack one medium-heavy coat that would suffice in cold weather for a while—just in case. I've worn mine one time in three years but think it is worth having. We each have lightweight jackets plus good rain gear. Our daily wear is jeans and polos. If you "layer" your clothing, packing an RV is the perfect place to practice. You can pack more actual pieces of clothing if you plan to wear it layered during colder weather.

Many people have some unusual clothing they want to take. For example, I take a tuxedo (yes, a real tux). We manage to take a cruise about once per year and I wear my tux for the formal nights on the cruise. It works for me. My joke is that the only time I wear a tie is when I'm on a cruise.

I also carry a blue blazer—another "just in case"—but rarely wear it. I can only recall being in one situation that required a jacket in the past six years. Dressing has become far more casual.

When we started fulltiming, we packed plenty of clothing that first year but as individual items wore out, they were tossed but not replaced. When we returned to our stored stuff the next year, we took more out of storage and continued tossing when appropriate.

We both are fairly traditional in our dress and do not necessarily follow the latest styles. We ended up with years of clothing accumulated in our closets when we were in our house. To initially move into the RV, we made multiple trips to donate clothing to a shelter. It took four years of fulltiming to wade through the remaining clothing in storage. We replaced worn-out items from storage when we returned each year.

The interesting thing about clothing while meandering about the country in an RV is that you could wear the exact same outfit every day and, with the exception of your spouse, no one would know. We continue today to toss but not replace clothing in an effort to reduce the total amount of clothing we carry. Hopefully, this newly acquired habit of simply owning and dealing with significantly less clothing will follow us should we choose to leave this lifestyle.

Shoes will likely be your biggest creative challenge when packing an RV. Because of their odd shapes, different styles, and different sizes (both men and women), they don't pack very well, take up lots of room, and using shoe boxes often consumes even more space (but they do stack well). Often, the best option is storing shoes in a plastic tub in the closet (if you have room.) Regardless, be selective.

Tools

Unfortunately, many individuals are known for their tool collection. Trust me on this… you do not have to take your garage full of tools in the RV. You will do some preventative maintenance but for the most part, you just can't handle heavy RV (truck chassis?) work on the side of the road. Most campgrounds won't let you work on your RV while parked on a site—they won't even let you change oil. Checking oil and fluids is usually the extent of what is allowed.

I recommend carrying one "small-but-normal" toolbox—just in case—with basic wrenches (metric and English), various screwdriver tips, Allen wrenches, and a general assortment of everything. You will need a caulking gun as RV caulk is a common companion. I also carry and recommend a good voltmeter.

For power tools, I have one small battery-powered drill with me but no other power tools. With the exception of one hacksaw, saws are totally unnecessary, most woodworking tools will be useless, and while air-powered tools could be powered from a large RV compressor, they, too, would be rarely used.

I carry tools I have never touched in our six years on the road—but not many now. This may be considered proof that some humans have the need to be close to tools even if they never use them. However, I do leave more in storage each time we return.

Kitchen/ Galley

Although your average RVer does not spend as much time in the RV galley as they do in a normal kitchen in their house, without question, an RV galley is important space. At minimum, eating in more often will cut costs to help offset higher fuel prices and other expenses. It is the kitchen where you can easily "remind" yourself of living in a house. You can prepare nearly all your favorite recipes. You will find, however, that guests in your RV will typically not gather in the kitchen/galley area like they do in a house.

Planning and packing an RV kitchen/galley consists of dealing with four groups of things: stuff you cook, stuff you cook it in, stuff that you cook with, and stuff you serve it on.

Food—Stuff You Cook

Simply stated, you will have to reduce the quantity of uncooked food you buy, the variety you typically stored at home, and the volume you occasionally prepare. You likely do not have room for lots of leftovers in an RV.

When we started fulltiming, we had lots (**lots!**) of canned and packaged goods from our home pantry. While living in a house, we had purchased in quantity, used one of those vacuum-sealing machines when buying in bulk, and shopped what we thought was normally.

To fit this into the RV, we first sorted out those canned and packaged foods used for our favorite recipes. From that, we packed a minimum number in the RV. For example, we have a favorite recipe that calls for one can of cream of chicken soup and we have this meal maybe once per month. So, we took just one can with us.

When we cook that recipe, we put cream of chicken soup on our shopping list and replace the one we used. This system works great.

Note that we replace the can **on the next shopping trip after we use it**. We do not wait until we are ready to prepare that recipe again and then have to go get the can of soup. Replacing foods immediately gives us more flexibility in the variety of meals we can prepare with food stored on board. Doing this also provides us with the ability to stop more places since we are not dependent on having to be someplace where we can purchase groceries locally.

One trick to prevent overbuying is to make your grocery list and put amounts on it. For example, rather than just listing "chicken soup" on the grocery list, put "1 can chicken soup" on it. Doing so will help prevent you from overbuying—regardless of that great sale price! Additionally, overbuying when living in an RV causes problems—where do you store it? We have seen RVers with food (canned goods) stored under the couch, over the bed, in the bathroom cabinets, in the shower, and even in their tow car! So the rule is: Don't buy it if it's not on the list.

Ultimately, to disperse the large quantity of leftover canned and packaged goods from our house, we told our (grown) family to help themselves. When we returned for a visit, they had gone through everything and then, we either took some more with us, tossed it (too old), or gave away the rest to a food bank.

A great way to "corral" those canned goods is to use lids from copy-paper boxes to organize and store canned goods in cabinets. The free lids are available at nearly every printer or copy shop. Slide the box lid into a pantry and it acts like a drawer. If your pantry shelf happens to be above your washer/dryer (as found in many motorhomes), two lids will fit side-by-side, i.e., two drawers. Doing so will buffer your canned goods while driving and they won't bounce around and beat up your shelf. You can simply grasp the lid and pull it toward you like a drawer to check your inventory in the rear.

Also, use the lids to carry canned goods to and from the house when packing/unpacking. If you don't like the looks of the lids, put some decorative contact paper on them.

Pots and Pans—Stuff You Cook It In

I cook the vast majority of our meals. I like my pots and pans and although we have good quality cookware, it is not a true "set" of cookware. I decided to only take those pots and pans that we really use.

You don't need lots of pots because most newer RVs have only three-burner or the now common two-burner stove top. Interestingly, the placement of the burners relative to each other on these stove tops will mandate the maximum size of your skillets. Typically, you cannot get two 12-inch skillets centered on the burners simultaneously on a two-burner stove top. The burners are too close together. Check this burner placement on any RV you may be planning to purchase especially if you are a serious cook and plan to prepare multiple-pot meals.

It's easy to sort out what to take with you since the RV stovetop and oven "sizes" will determine the size of pots and pans you can take and use effectively.

I have one large Dutch oven and one large stock pot. If necessary, store large pots in your underneath storage compartments. Since you rarely need them, this works well. If a pot is too large to easily wash in the galley sink—wash it in the shower. If you do this, be sure to clean up any greasy residue left on the floor of the shower stall.

Domed lids are great for cooking but hard to pack. We put those in storage and replaced them with flat lids (available from any restaurant supply and inexpensive). These work great for cooking and are a breeze to store.

Another great pot for RV use is the traditional pressure cooker. There are four reasons for this…

- You can cook delicious meals much faster in the pressure cooker and therefore, use less fuel.

- Having the pressure cooker available provides you with another excellent large cooking pot to use normally—not just as a pressure cooker.

- You cook one-pot meals and this eliminates lots of extra clean-up when boondocking.

- You can cook more efficiently if you are parked at higher altitudes. The reason is that water boils at a lower temperature (less than 212° F) at the higher altitudes. Therefore, traditional cooking (not in a pressure cooker) will take longer since the water is actually cooler. After all, you can't avoid Denver forever.

We have two of the CorningWare® bowls that are oven/freezer/stove-top safe and work well. These must be protected when traveling as they can break.

Some companies have released "nesting" cookware that is functional, appropriate for RVs, and looks good. The handles are removable and the pots/skillets "nest"—i.e. are stored inside each other. A whole set of pots and pans may be stored inside one 8-quart pot.

When packing an RV, you always have to consider vibrations. Everything in the RV vibrates when going down the highway or even when the engine is just idling. Usually, nothing vibrates sitting in your pantry at home. Therefore, you must remember to protect your non-stick cookware when traveling in your RV. If non-stick cookware is nested (like a typical baking pan or cookie sheet) and there is any potential for something rubbing against it, the non-stick cook surface will rub through and ruin the cookware.

Silicone Bakeware... The silicone bakeware is an RVers dream product. Commonly found at a variety of stores today, this is weird stuff—silicone bakeware doesn't act or feel normal. Many people don't trust it. That makes sense—I didn't trust it either, at first.

Silicone bakeware was developed in the 1980s for commercial kitchens. It is FDA approved, inert, and safe up to various high temperatures (stamped in the silicone of each piece). Silicone will melt if heated above its safe range but even then, doesn't produce toxic vapors. Silicone cookware includes muffin pans, baking pans, spatulas, molds, whisks, and more. It is the only non-reactive, non-stick cooking material.

Silicone bakeware is great anywhere but is considered "the answer" for RVers. It is…

- **Flexible**. You can literally roll your silicone bakeware or just wad it up and stuff it in a drawer. You can use it as a cushion to pack between other conventional pans for travel. It will fit and can be tucked in just about anywhere.

- **Lightweight**. My guess is that silicone bakeware is about 1/10 the weight of its counterpart glass baking dishes. Regardless of the actual amount, it is significantly less weight. Leave those glass baking dishes behind.

- **Cooks Great**. Use silicone bakeware in any appliance where it will **not come in contact with direct heat** (like an open flame or electric burner). Also, you cannot put it under a broiler. It's great in microwave, conventional gas or electric ovens, and convection ovens. Don't change your recipe times or temperatures when cooking with silicone.

- **Easy to Clean**. I always oil my silicone bakeware with a bit of olive oil. Even so, while it's the best non-stick material I've used, occasionally food will stick. Since it's flexible, just bend the pan and the residual food often pops off! Wash it with the other dishes. It is also dishwasher safe.

- **Cheap**. Don't pay big bucks for silicone—shop around. We paid $19.00 (yes, nineteen) for a three-piece set (loaf pan, Bundt pan, and muffin pan) of silicone cookware at a pharmacy chain. It works great!

Sharp objects like knives or forks can damage silicon bakeware. If you happen to cut, but not pierce a hole in the piece, the pan is still usable but food will collect and stick inside the cut. To help p r e v e n t accidently cutting my silicone bakeware, I use  silicone spatulas. Metal forks and sharp knives can puncture this cookware and render it useless. Also be careful when putting the silicone bakeware in the dishwater with sharp objects. I think it is best to wash the knives and forks first and get them out of the sink before putting in your silicone bakeware.

The flexibility of silicone also works against you when trying to carry any liquids. Try filling a 9 x 13-inch silicone baking pan with a runny batter and then put it in the oven! It's hard enough with a metal or glass dish. A floppy pan brings on new challenges.

For baking, our convection oven requires a metal rack that sits on the microwave tray. I set my 9 x 13 silicone pan on this rack, pour in the batter, and then lift the metal rack (with silicone baking pan on it) up into the oven. This provides some stability to the liquid batter in the pan. Or, place your silicone cookware on a cookie sheet and when filled, lift the cookie sheet and slide the bakeware into the oven.

Silicone bakeware is nearly the perfect product for RVers. While it won't make your food taste better, it will make it a bit more fun to cook and an absolute breeze to store the cookware.

Utensils & Appliances—Stuff You Cook With

We have the normal array of kitchen tools, utensils, and (limited) gadgets with us but not as much as we had in our house. One "habit" that is common while living in a house is that everyone tends to collect kitchen gadgets. Granted, they may work fine but you may only use them once every year or so. Sorry, you will have to sort through these before packing the RV. The drawer storage in most RV galleys is extremely limited. With that, I recommend that unless you actually prepare apples frequently, perhaps you should leave that counter-mounted apple-peeler-corer in storage.

Large kitchen appliances are really difficult to take, store, and use in a typical RV galley. There's just not enough work room and counter space. Appliances such as the large counter-top mixers, blenders, rice cookers, and food processors simply won't fit on the counter (work surface) and leave any room to do other work. Another unusual space limitation is the short vertical height between the counter top and the upper cabinets (or bottom of the microwave since many manufacturers locate them above the cook stove). This vertical clearance will also limit your using the taller, counter-top appliances. Lots of RVers do use the slow-cooker type of appliance. This is totally a personal choice.

If you insist on taking and using large kitchen appliances, you have two choices when cooking...

- Pull the large appliances out of the pantry (or wherever you store them in your RV), use them for food preparation, and immediately clean and put them away.

- Use the large appliances on the dining table (But doing this creates a potential for making a mess carrying things back and forth because the dining table is almost always on the opposite side of the coach from the stove top).

My recommendation is to leave your large kitchen appliances in long-term storage and don't take them with you. Replace that big counter-top mixer with a very small hand-held one.

Unfortunately, when you first looked at that RV and decided to purchase it, the cooktop and sink was likely covered with matching covers that gave the impression of a very decent-size work surface like the one shown here.

[The galley slide **closed**—ready to drive.]

I'm sorry, but you must remove the cooktop covers to actually cook! As a result of removing them, you may reduce your actual counter-top working area by half or more! Then, you may also have to remove your sink covers when starting to cook (washing, peeling vegetables, etc.). Doing this will reduce your actual work area even further.

[**Author note**: Whenever you seriously look at an RV, always remove the sink and stove covers while you look around. How much actual work surface do you have? Where can you store the covers when parked a few days? Compare the "real" space you can actually use without the sink and stove covers but with a couple of appliances setting out. You don't want to discover this after you drive away in your new RV.]

[The galley slide **open**—parked.]

Remember, when RVing, you are likely cooking for two, not a group. Even the occasional shared meal (like potluck gatherings) often limit you to preparing one dish. Doing this may require larger pots/pans but not more of them. You will rarely need those large mixers, blenders, and food processors in an RV environment where you are frequently traveling.

Dishes & Glassware—Stuff You Serve It On

Keep your glassware to a minimum. Remember, you can feed six inside a big RV with a sit-down dinner but everyone will have to compromise and adjust a bit. Eight will fit inside for drinks and appetizers so long as some people are standing. It would be rare that you would entertain a group and RVers typically bring their own drinks with them. Therefore, glassware can be kept at a minimum.

We have six very nice, stemmed, crystal wine glasses with us. It's a nice touch to bring them out occasionally. We once served champagne and strawberries by the campfire. We store these by tucking them in foam-rubber drink huggies. Coffee cups are a personal choice. I like the plastic ones that don't drip. We keep throwaway plastic cups on board.

All this stuff vibrates when going down the highway and even when just sitting and the engine is idling. Plastic is always better, easier to pack for travel, and certainly more safe than glassware.

One source for relatively tough plastic dishes and glasses is any store that stocks "pool ware." These dishes are nonbreakable and sold nearly every place that handles swimming pool supplies.

Dishes often lend a feeling of some permanence— maybe even a touch of elegance. We are really not "roughing" it. Some fulltimers told us they tried using paper plates all the time but it gets tiresome.

I always recommend carrying decent quality paper plates as they are great for boondocking. Also purchase the better-quality plastic, disposable tableware in bulk (about 120 each of the knife, fork, and spoon and available from the big-box stores). Don't get the cheap, flimsy stuff. Typically, you will use up spoons the slowest. To balance this, we use spoons instead of knives to spread condiments—for example, when we are making a sandwich.

I recommend having some of the "Corelle" type dishes for daily use. They travel well, are really tough, nearly impossible to break, easy to wash, are oven and freezer proof, and make the meal a bit more elegant because you are actually using glass dishes—not paper or plastic. Remember, this is your home so act like it!

We normally use the glass products (dishes and glasses/cups) when hooked up to shore power and use the paper/plastic (throwaway) when boondocking. It works for us. We are concerned with the environment but feel the occasional use of throwaway products is easily justified by our lifestyle.

Don't Forget the Clean-up... Fulltiming in an RV may cause your normal "home" kitchen clean-up process to be a bit different. Regardless of your normal after-the-meal-clean-up process in your house, it will have to be done after every major meal in the RV. There are two reasons for this. First, there just isn't extra room to accumulate stacks of dirty dishes plus cooking utensils. Second, since you have likely limited the amount of dishes and cooking utensils packed in your RV, you simply won't have more to use without first cleaning up.

Outdoor Things

There are a few common outdoor items to carry with you when RVing. These are typically carried in the various compartments around the RV and accessible from the outside. Some type of grill is likely the most common. Chairs are nice and handy. Plus everyone needs a ladder on occasion.

Caution! **Do not buy this stuff until you have the RV.** Otherwise, they might not fit. By having the RV first, you can immediately check to see if any particular item will store underneath for travel. You cannot guess at the size of your underneath storage compartments.

Grills… There are two kinds: gas and charcoal briquette. Due to the potential dangers of open flames and unattended fires, many/most RV parks, state, and federal parks allow gas grills only. Open fires, if allowed, are often confined to a "fire ring"—a designated spot for the campfire.

While there are advantages to both types of grills, the important issue here is size. Sorry, but you cannot take that patio-sized monster that will hold 50 hamburger patties! If you insist, talk to some tailgaters! You may want to search for a smaller grill but do not buy it until you actually have the RV.

It is rare to find a free-standing grill (such as one typically sitting on a patio) in an RV. These types of grills are just too large to store. If you see these larger grills, and they are most common at the classic tailgate gatherings, they are usually owned by part-time RVers—not fulltimers. Most of the grills that fulltimers use are the table-top variety simply because of the space they consume.

Chairs… You will see a variety of chairs including the lawn chairs/chaise lounges/camping chairs/stools at various RV gatherings. It seems everyone has them. You will need one for each person traveling with you but no extra. For example, if just you and your spouse travel alone, then take two chairs. RVers will naturally bring their own chairs to any gathering as this is the generally accepted practice in RV etiquette. You are not expected to furnish outdoor chairs for others. However, your non-RVing visitors will not be aware of this practice. So, when they visit, bring out the chairs from the galley or use the picnic table.

Some outdoor chairs fold very thin and are easy to store underneath. Some of the chaise lounges are quite bulky and take up ample room. No matter what

sale you found, as with the grills, wait on the purchase of these chairs until you are relatively comfortable with the other items that have to go underneath. Then purchase the chairs to fit the storage space available. The alternative is to have to rearrange things underneath so the chairs will fit. Remember, your space is finite.

If you are a fan of the potluck dinners that are common among RVers, you might want to consider the type of chairs that have the small shelf on one side. When the chair is opened for seating, the shelf can be raised and locked into position. The chair and the shelf is sturdy and just the right size to hold a tray of food. The chair can be used with the shelf in the folded-down position.

Folding Table… Many RVers carry a folding table for outdoor use and numerous sizes, kinds, and styles are available. The smaller tables will be about the same size as a small end table. These work well to hold one tray of food. Several sizes are available—ours is 30 inches X 48 inches making it large enough for four people to sit down for a meal. It folds up to a compact tube-type "package" that is 48 inches long and about 8 inches in diameter making it easy to carry and easy to store in our coach.

I also recommend the type of table with the top that literally rolls up—not a rigid table that folds in half. While these rigid tables are sturdy, they are sometimes difficult to fit underneath in your storage compartments. Sometimes, you may be able to store and hide one of the rigid, folding tables behind your couch. There may be a gap between the couch and wall of the coach where it will fit. It may also fit if your couch unfolds into a bed.

One unusual note regarding selecting your folding table is that many have one fold-down leg on each end—it looks like a giant letter "U"—and each end folds down. The part of the leg sitting on the ground (the bottom of the "U") must be on a fairly flat surface or the table will be wobbly. I recommend a table with any type of legs where only four points (legs) actually touch the ground. It's much easier to level. Much of your use will likely be on an unlevel surface.

Granted, most campsites will have the typical picnic table on the site. Some are concrete monsters that are unmovable. Some are so rickety that you wouldn't take a chance and use them. Some are fine. With the variety and condition that we have found traveling everywhere, I recommend you carry your own folding table—just to be on the safe side. That way, you will have one when you need it.

One use for the folding table is for participating in any gathering. RVers will take their chairs and often be asked to lend their table if it is appropriate. A few of these tables pushed together will hold lots of food goodies.

Ladder... Of the various types of ladders, the ones that fold up into some small "package" are popular among RVers since they are easy to store—usually underneath.

I absolutely refuse to bungee cord some 8-foot orange or blue ladder to the rear of my motorhome. I think it looks like Jed Clampitt just drove into town (sorry, Jed) with this hanging on the rear of a $150,000 or $350,000 motorhome! Plus, it never matches my exterior color scheme anyway! My ladder is always going to be stored out of sight.

Look long and hard at the many different types of ladders available today. Some will telescope, others will fold into a long, small rectangle (it stores and looks like a fence post), still others fold flat and really thin and have real steps, not rungs. A visit to the huge hardware centers will be an eye opener. Also ask to see what they can order.

When you choose your ladder, make sure you can store it with whatever other items you have. A ladder always has such an unusual shape that it is not easy to fit into an underneath storage compartment especially if yours is pretty full of other really important stuff.

[**A Safety Note**: Every ladder has weight limits and you must be aware of these. Don't plan to climb a ladder that is not designed to hold your weight. By law, the weight limit is posted on the label and you should trust it. Most inexpensive ladders will have a lighter weight limit. Check for your own safety.]

What Else Do We Need To Know

Where is Home Base

All fulltimers need a "home base." A home base is not necessarily your home. It is roughly defined as some location you occasionally or regularly return to for any number of reasons. For example, most of your family may live there, your medical contacts and history (doctors, dentist, others) might be in one local area, it could be where your house is/was located, or, like us, all of the above. Some potential and new fulltimers insist on keeping their house and that can be their home base. Some use relatives (we use our daughter's house)—not as a place we live but just for mailing and a place we visit occasionally. Your domicile (legal address) and your mailing address can be in different states. Interestingly, both these addresses could be different from your home base.

> *A Personal Story... We are constantly asked "Where are you from?" or "Where is your home?" Our usual answer is "Our last house was in Texas." because we had lived there 16 years when we sold it and started fulltiming. It works.*
>
> *The ongoing and overused "joke" answer to questions like, "Where is your home?" is to say, "Here in the Wal-Mart parking lot." or some such nonsense. RVers have heard this a thousand times and non-RVers won't understand it.*

Legal Residence

It is common for fulltimers to change their domicile (legal address) to another state. One common reason is state tax. Seven states have **no state income tax**—Alaska, Florida, Nevada, South Dakota, Texas, Washington, and Wyoming. Five states have **no sales tax**—Alaska, Delaware, Montana, New Hampshire, and Oregon. Note: Alaska is the only state that does not have either tax.

The question often asked is which is more important, sales or state income tax. That can only be answered by you and your personal financial situation. Contact your CPA and talk it over based on your future earnings and planned expenditures.

As a fulltimer, you live in your RV, your domicile (legal address) is used for voter registration and driver's license. As previously stated, your legal address may be different from your mailing address. Review the section on *"Regular Mail"* in the chapter entitled, *"How Do We Stay In Touch"* for a complete discussion of mailing addresses and services.

Creating an LLC

RVers and others are known to set up a Limited Liability Corporation (LLC) in states that have no sales tax. Actually, LLCs can be formed in all fifty states. Then, when purchasing the RV (or boat, or "big ticket" items), the LLC does the purchase (the RV belongs to the corporation) and also licenses the vehicle. To restate… the RV belongs to and is licensed to the corporation. The LLC is a legal entity in a given state. If that state does not have a sales tax, then there is no sales tax on any purchase by the LLC.

Financing the purchase may be more difficult since not all banks will make the loan to the LLC. Additionally, RVers may find themselves with a domicile (legal address) plus driver's license in one state and driving a vehicle with a license plate from another state. Other examples are driving an RV licensed in one state and towing a vehicle licensed in another state.

RVers interested in pursuing this as an option should do their research carefully. You can visit with companies offering this service (setting up an LLC) at various large RV rallies and shows. You should talk with other RVers who have gone through this experience. As with any legal questions, speak with your attorney.

Where Can We Go

New fulltimers are similar to balls-in-play on a pinball machine. You know, the ones where the steel balls kind of bounce all over the place—ka-bing, ka-bing, ka-bing! Typically new fulltimers will travel like that—from here to there then over there and back here! They are having fun, have the flexibility, want to see it all, and it's tough to not go. After all, isn't that why we are fulltiming? The longer you fulltime, the slower you tend to go—not in speed, but in time. No matter how fast you go, you can't see it all. Sorry.

A Personal Story… We were in Laramie, Wyoming and ultimately were headed to Illinois but had plenty of time. I think it was my brilliant idea to go through Yellowstone National Park (also in Wyoming) on the way back to Illinois.

It's 450 miles northwest of Laramie into Yellowstone National Park—away from Illinois. So, 900 miles later, we were really on our way home to Illinois.

There are two types of fulltimers. There are those with specific destinations in mind with a plan to get there and stay for some period of time. The classic "snowbird" is this type. The other type loves to "meander," that is, just sort of go all over the place, stopping wherever the urge strikes, staying a few days, then moving on, and sometimes driving out of the campground and asking, "Do you want to turn left or right?" We do this all the time.

All fulltimers have to discover their personal style of travel. Ours is that we meander to what I will call "areas"—an example is the northwest Pacific coast or the Canadian Maritimes. We may have some specific reason for going there (a rally, family visit, or some special event) but we take advantage of the travel route getting there and then staying there to explore. We never try nor intend to see it all as that would likely require us to live there permanently for some extended period.

USA

You just cannot see it all. You cannot. It's too big. There are too many places. There's not enough time. Sorry. But that's part of what makes it great, too. So do what you can while you can.

We have had the good fortune to visit all the states several times each. No, we did not drive the RV to Hawaii (some say this will cause it to rust). Granted, some places are not as exciting as others but every state has unique things to see and do.

RVers have their own travel style and you will, too. Some crisscross a state like a search grid, trying to see everything before going to the next state. Others drive miles out of their way just to touch the corner of some state so they can color in that US map pasted on the side of their coach and can say, "Yes, we have been in ???". Some follow historical routes. Three popular routes are Route 66, the Natchez Trace, and the Lewis and Clark Route. Other RVers plan their travel to sites based on historical events such as civil war battlegrounds, western forts, or reconstructed villages. Some RVers follow major rivers while some just visit their children. Regardless of your style, you just cannot see it all.

There are some places in the USA that you cannot drive or tow a big rig due to the condition of the highways. For example, California posts a list of their restricted highways. You should check carefully before getting too far off any normal route.

I stumbled onto one of the California restricted routes once. This was a totally innocent decision on our part—we just wanted to drive along the coast a bit and this route was a two-lane, n u m b e r e d highway. That ended up being  one of the toughest drives I have ever made in a motorhome. My coach was just too big for the road and I ended up scraping a guardrail trying to avoid a log truck while going around a switchback. I was going really slow and being careful but there just wasn't room to maneuver.

Canada

We love traveling in Canada. There are wonderful and unique sights that are not available anywhere else. The food, the people, Canadian highways, and RV-related facilities are, for the most part, excellent. We have had the good fortune to travel extensively from Detroit, east to Toronto, Montreal, Quebec City, up the St. Lawrence, down to New Brunswick, on to Prince Edward Island, Nova Scotia, and finally back into Maine. Another trip took us north from North Dakota to Regina, Saskatchewan and west to the Canadian Rockies (near Calgary), into the park to Banff, north to Lake Louise, across the Columbia Ice Fields, then Jasper, and out of the park southwest to Vancouver, British Columbia. Both were great trips. We allocated about eight weeks for the Canadian portion of each trip. We also spent a few weeks in Canada going to and from Alaska.

Traveling in Canada now requires a passport to cross the border **both ways**—don't leave home without it. You may have your RV searched trying to enter the country—don't carry any contraband or weapons, period.

Alaska

Alaska is considered the ultimate destination for RVers. Visiting a place over twice the size of Texas having only three cities with over 10,000 population, and having your "home" with you just makes sense as accommodations are not always near where you want to be. There are limits as to when you can take an RV there and the suggested time is to be south of Whitehorse, Yukon Territory, Canada **before Memorial Day and after Labor Day** to avoid snowstorms.

An average Alaska trip in an RV is going to be in the range of 10,000–12,000 miles. The three ways to get there:

- Caravan (with an RV tour company)
- Alaska Marine Ferry (drive your RV off at most stops, stay for a few days, and reboard)
- On your own.

The major RV magazines regularly offer articles on travel to Alaska. It is easy to find (sometimes too much) information about any aspect of that trip. Seminars focusing on Alaskan travel are also common at rallies. It is an RVer's dream trip.

We made the Alaskan trip in 2008 on our own. That trip and the many differences and uniqueness of RVing in northern Canada and Alaska is in my book, *"RVing to Alaska"* released January 2010. <**aboutrving.com**>

Other Places

We have never taken an RV into Mexico but many others have and do so regularly. I talked with one couple that actually drove their RV to somewhere in South America (sorry, I don't remember where) and another that drove theirs from the Arctic Circle to the Panama Canal. If you choose to venture south, do your research and find out the rules, regulations, and potential pitfalls long before starting out.

How Can We Get There

RVers are an unusual bunch. Some want to travel alone, period. Others won't go anyplace without a group. Plus, you can go with a large group or a small one. You have total flexibility and can always travel by whatever method suits you best.

Commercial Tours or Caravans

There are several private companies that conduct planned, organized trips specifically for RVers. You must have an RV, pay their fee, and the trip is done with a "wagon master" (tour leader) and other RVers. Another common option is to simply meet at a destination and stay for a predetermined time. Everything is planned and you are with an experienced tour guide who shares your interest in RVing.

Caravans are one type where part of the trip is the actual driving to some destination—the drive is part of the daily scheduled activity. Alaska is one of the most popular driving tours for caravans. Caravans often provide flexibility in daily departure times. For example, many caravans require you to leave between 6:30 and 9:30 AM. Most events and campsites are scheduled so you must arrive at the daily destination by a certain time. If you leave earlier, you have more time during the day to stop and mess around. Longer caravans have a "tail gunner" who always assumes the position of last RV. Often, the tail gunner can provide light emergency service—or get professional help—if an RV is disabled along the way.

CB-radio communication is common in caravans and small groups may hear a verbal "travel" dialogue through certain areas. Some caravans may load onto a ferry or rail flatcar and unload some distance away. Your route, daily itinerary, "tourist" stops, campgrounds, and some meals are carefully planned by the tour company. You pay a fee and abide by their schedule and route.

For other RV tours, you do not drive there together but just meet at some prearranged place (like a campground) for a special event. Two popular events for this type of tour are the Albuquerque Balloon Festival and Tournament of Roses Parade in Pasadena, California. We did the Rose Parade with an RV tour company. It was an excellent experience and I recommend it.

Both caravans and tours may, at first, seem expensive. However, check thoroughly into the total trip before judging it. It is common for the tour companies to schedule lots of catered meals, numerous smaller side tours, and a variety of activities as part of the total tour "package." If you separately priced everything included in the tour package, you may be getting a real value. That's the good news. The other news is that you may not care about all those scheduled activities. If this is not your style of travel, don't go.

Small Groups

It is common for small groups of RVers to travel together. Since three large RVs can require lots of parking space, when traveling in groups of more than three, simple plans such as stopping for lunch can be a real challenge. However, three RVs (assuming six people) is the perfect number for gathering. You can do a sit-down dinner for six inside an RV although it requires a bit of special effort from everyone—but feeding eight (assuming there are four RVs in your small group) is nearly impossible unless it's just standing around munching appetizers. You cannot plan on being outside every evening.

Some older campgrounds may have just a few spaces that will accommodate large rigs. Calling for reservations for three large rigs will limit where you can stay. I would strongly recommend calling ahead.

We always recommend and literally talk over some "ground rules" when planning to travel with others. While these, at first, may seem somewhat blunt, they work, and no one will have their feelings hurt later. Here are some we use and you can add your own. None of these are meant to take personally…

- We don't have to get together and visit every night. Sometimes we want to be alone. So if we turn you down when you ask if we want to go out to eat, or come over, or sit by the fire, don't take it personally or get insulted. Conversely, we won't when you turn us down.

- Bring your drinks with you. Don't expect us to carry a variety of drinks for everyone—we don't have room. Whether for a happy hour or a meal, bring your own drinks. Of course, if I buy a special bottle of wine (or anything) and invite you to share it, that's different and is usually for a special occasion.

- If we are gathering outside, bring your chairs. We carry two. That's a perfect match since we have two people living in our coach. We don't carry seating for others.

- When planning to cook and eat together, agree up front if one couple will provide the entire meal or it's to be potluck. If we agreed that I would provide the entire meal, don't "surprise" me by bringing something. Since I didn't plan for it, I likely don't have room for it, and it may not even fit on the table. Remember, we are eating in an RV.

- Don't assume that if you invite me, I will bring something. I won't unless you ask. Please don't hesitate to ask. I enjoy helping.

- When driving down the highway, if someone wants to stop (for whatever reason), we stop.

- If you have no interest in visiting a particular tourist stop, say so. If I do want to visit it, I will say so, too. We can stop, we will go in, you can wait, come in, or drive on.

- It's okay to part for a few hours or a few days and plan to get back together later. You may want to stay longer than we do in a particular area.

- Let's agree on a speed to drive. The lead driver can change this temporarily when conditions warrant it.

- Let's agree on a route. If something comes up, we can change this during the day and the lead driver will have to choose the way if needed.

- Let's agree on some approximate destination or number of miles for the day. This, of course, is changeable.

- Choose the lead driver based on their ability to judge RV maneuvering and parking. They have to have a pretty good "feel" for the space needed for all the coaches when pulling into or having to get out of some parking area.

- If you are the lead driver, drive with the cruise control. I don't care if you are convinced that you can hold a steady speed, you cannot match the steadiness of a cruise control.

- Let's agree on a time to leave in the morning. (Note: Be careful here. If one couple is an early riser and the other is a typical late morning pair —the relationship will likely not work for long. You must be relatively compatible.)

- Let's agree to pay for our own meals as we go. It eliminates the unnecessary haggling. We will ask the waitstaff to split the check accordingly.

Some compromise and flexibility on the part of everyone is the key to a successful trip. Agreeing on some/most of these "rules" just makes sense. However, traveling in a small group provides numerous advantages. You can check on, help, and watch out for each other.

Travel Alone

You are never actually alone if traveling with a spouse. We are perfectly content to travel—and have done so extensively—without the daily company of others. But, we have also traveled with other RVers and had a wonderful time. When traveling alone, there are the obvious advantages of not having to discuss with others what you would like to do with the hope that they will enjoy the same type of adventures as you. A single RV has much more flexibility in stopping/parking temporarily (for lunch, tours, campground, whatever).

There are areas, especially northern Canada and Alaska, where I believe it would be best to travel with one or two other RVers both for safety and potential mechanical problems.

RV Etiquette

Universally, RVers are known for their friendliness. For some unknown reason, RVers will simply gather naturally and the conversation starts. Some joke that since you spend so much time in a confined space with your spouse, you can't wait to get out and talk to someone/anyone else! Regardless, RVers are a friendly bunch. You will see, time and again, a $500,000 motorhome pull into a campsite next to a $25,000 travel trailer and even before hooking up, the conversation has started.

Rules of RV Etiquette

There are some "rules" of etiquette that are unique to RVing. Here are a few common ones...

- Don't walk through campsites. You are welcome to come on site to knock on our door but just like the last neighborhood you lived in, strangers did not normally just walk through your property up close to your house. The campsite is temporarily my property as I'm renting it for the night.

- If my shades are closed, please don't knock unless it is an emergency or we have invited you over. This applies 24/7.

- You can hear outside sounds from inside virtually all RVs. I know you paid a lot for that big outdoor TV in your front storage compartment. Don't assume we want to hear it. Do assume we can hear it. I can close my shades to block the view but not the sound. Remember, your TV/CD/whatever player is right outside my living room.

- Don't assume everyone likes your pet.

- Don't ever bring your pet into our coach unless we discussed it first.

- If you are a smoker, do not smoke in our RV. Even if you ask permission, we will say no. Don't take it personally, we say no to everyone who asks.

- If you are a smoker, please do not smoke near our RV. If we have our windows open and our ceiling fans on, we will suck the secondhand smoke into our coach. That's not something we want to have happen.

- We would appreciate it if you would not idle your RV (diesel pusher or tow vehicle) for very long when you pull out of the campground before the crack of dawn!

- If you see something wrong with my RV or my utility connections, please tell me. I will fix it if possible.

- If we are going to sit outside, bring your chairs.

- Other than the chairs and grill sitting out, don't store stuff outside by sticking it under your RV. It looks trashy. I see it from our RV. You cannot see it from inside your RV.

- If you are invited inside and see shoes sitting near the door, we would prefer you take yours off, too. Take the hint.

- Don't ask to see inside. This is our home. If we want you to see it, first, we must be comfortable enough that we will ask you in. If we do invite you in, you will likely get the tour.

Campground Laundry

The campground laundromat is a nice convenience for RVers. There are far more RVs without a washer/dryer on board than there are with one. Therefore, campground laundry facilities are important to a lot of people.

While you may have a "combo" washer/dryer in your coach, access to the larger "home" machines is handy especially when washing heavy items like throw rugs or blankets. [Note: Purchase a copy of *"Wrinkle-Free RV Laundry"* to learn all the secrets of using the combo washer/dryer. Available at <aboutrving.com>]

Campground laundromats are typically small—often with maybe just a couple of machines. Therefore, some "rules" of etiquette should be followed...

- Don't start your laundry and leave since they may only have one or two machines.
- Don't wash really filthy stuff - pet hair, sand, mud, grease.
- Don't put anything in campground machines that you wouldn't put in yours at home.
- Wipe up after yourself. There is typically no attendant on duty for the campground laundry.
- Use a damp cloth and wipe out the machine when finished if there is a lot of pet hair or lint.

Campground laundromats are also excellent places for meeting other RVers and exchanging information. You may also find a paperback book exchange. Plus, if you still use a modem connection for getting online, the campground laundromat is a common place to find the phone line (jack) connection. You usually have to take your own phone cord.

RV Events

Rallies

An RV rally is a planned gathering of RVers with something in common. This could be an association or club membership (Good Sam and FMCA are the two largest), the brand of RV (an "owner's rally"), or a dealership hosting previous customers.

Rallies take place all the time, nationwide, are a great way to meet other RVers, obtain information, see accessories, obtain warranty—sometimes even out-of-warranty—service, and see some good entertainment. Your rally fees usually cover everything including on-site parking for your coach. We've attended rallies with 5–10 RVs and others with over 5,000 coaches.

Good Sam and FMCA conduct huge national/international rallies annually. For example, "The Rally," one of the largest has hosted about 4,000+ RVs. A rally this size requires lots of planning to keep you busy and happy. The planning for these starts years in advance.

Here are typical "normal" activities ongoing during a rally...

Seminars... Are presented on all things RV such as driving, cooking, safety, cleaning, maintenance, tours, costs, RV resorts, fulltiming, tires, and many others. It's a great way to get updated information about

RVing. Use your best judgement to determine if the seminar is just another product infomercial or truly an educational seminar. If you don't like it, walk out. It's your time.

Vendors… Will set up their booths—usually inside a building—and sell all things RV from tow bars to sewer hoses to books to insurance. We are vendors and sell our books at rallies. Meander through the vendors and talk with them. It's a great way to keep current on new innovations in RVing.

One unusual hint is that you should consider purchasing products **early** in the rally. If there are problems, you can easily return the product to the vendor. Or, if you are confused about the operation of your new purchase, you have time to visit with the vendor. Visit the vendors two or three times to reduce information overload from one giant visit. As with all retail sales, there will be some true gadgets. Never forget: Caveat emptor… *"Let the buyer beware."*

Dealers… Bring in new RVs to display and sell. They will wheel-and-deal on the spot and you can actually drive one home. We have seen people actually move into a new coach while the rally was going on.

Maintenance/Repair… May be offered by RV manufacturers and after-market companies. They occasionally bring service technicians and lots of common replacement parts to the rally. You must sign up for the service, the technician shows up, and does the work—if possible. Major repairs cannot be done. The general "rule" is that the repair should take less than an hour. I have had Monaco, Blue Ox, and MotoSAT work done at a rally. You meet them and unlock your coach if needed. Blue Ox checked, updated, and lubricated my tow bar and I wasn't there. The good news is there frequently is no charge for this on-site and excellent customer service!

Entertainment... Is offered nearly every night and it's excellent. The larger rallies bring in the bigger stars. You will have fun.

Tours... There are always local tours.

Food... Is everywhere. The ice cream social is the most popular. Some rallies offer meals as part of the "package." Regardless, you won't go hungry.
Especially at smaller rallies, the potluck meals are always in season.

Or, you can just sit around and wave at other RVers walking by! From potluck gatherings to entertainment, participation in any of the planned events is never mandatory and you do what you want to do.

Statewide Good Sam rallies are called "Samborees." Also, local Good Sam chapters—based on geographical areas or interests —frequently get together. There are many local chapter rallies. Find this information at <**goodsamclub.com**>. Look for "RV Events & Tours."

FMCA sponsors "Area" rallies and draw from a broader, multi-state geographical area. FMCA also has hundreds of local chapters and activities. Find this information at <fmca.com> and look under "Conventions" and "Chapters/Areas."

RV manufacturers and dealers also sponsor rallies. For example, Monaco sponsors 15 different RV clubs just for specific Monaco-brand owners. Some are geographical memberships while others are limited to specific models of coaches. Look at <monacocoach.com/owners/clubs.html>.

RV Shows

Dealers and vendors gather at RV shows to display and sell their products. Like any show, you must pay an entrance fee. This allows you to browse through the products, see the latest innovations, and talk with sales reps. Long before you make that purchase, attending RV shows is an excellent way to do some research and get information. Two particular shows have a large attendance—Tampa, FL and Hershey, PA—each has about 40,000 attendees. While large crowds may not interest you, the largest selection of new RVs and products will be displayed at the largest shows. Don't miss the smaller shows, too. Most major cities will have an RV show sometime during the year.

Continue attending your local RV shows after your purchase. You'll get ideas, see new products, purchase accessories, and get the latest information. Plus, it's cheap entertainment.

Boondocking

You have purchased a vehicle or unit that is self-contained—that is, you have the ability to live in it for some period of time without hooking up to utilities (electric, water, and sewer). The permanent-type of hookup where the RV utilities are connected is commonly called "shore power" (a term borrowed from the boating industry). With the normal systems on-board your RV, you can boondock (stay one or two nights) or dry camp (stay several nights) without hooking up to shore power. It is important to note that you do not have to deprive yourself of anything while boondocking. You live with the same comfort and convenience as you do when hooked up. We definitely do not "rough it." Our definition of "roughing it" is if the wine is not perfectly chilled!

Part of being able to live in the unit without being plugged into shore power is accomplished by an alternative electrical source on board. You likely have special "coach" batteries that will run most of the electrical things you need to live normally. The batteries will not run high-amperage-draw appliances like your air conditioners, hair dryer, microwave oven, or toaster oven. It is also common to have a generator that, when running, will furnish electricity to those high-amperage-draw appliances plus charge the coach batteries. Nearly all Class A motorhomes have a generator.

Some Class C units may not have a generator. Travel trailers and 5th wheel units often do not have a generator. You can easily add one by purchasing a portable generator. Depending on its size and capacity, it may fit in a storage compartment or, commonly, in the bed of the pick-up used to pull the RV. These portable units work fine. You will have to monitor and limit your appliance usage to not exceed the capacity of the generator. Additionally, you will have to know how much noise your generator actually puts out. Some RV parking places may have a maximum decibel limit for a running generator. Additionally, nearly all places will have a "quiet time" when all generators are to be shut down.

The other part of being able to live in the your RV without hooking up is accomplished by your RV water system including "holding tanks." These are large plastic tanks and most RVs have three—one for fresh water (potable, or "drinking" water), one for "grey" water (the runoff from all sinks and shower drains), and one for "black" water (sewage). Thus, with your RV's built-in electrical and water systems, you can live comfortably not hooked up to shore power.

We regularly boondock. We do this due to convenience —whenever it is easy to do and cost savings does not enter our decision. Of course there is a cost savings but the convenience is absolutely wonderful. For example, I would hate to really want to stop (tired, sleepy, hungry, whatever) and have to drive another 40 miles to my campground. That's just not safe either. We averaged boondocking 11 nights per month during 2006 and 12 nights per month 2007 through 2010.

I am not "anti-campground." When I need those things (utilities and space) a campground offers, I pay their fee, stay there, and appreciate the opportunity. Consider this... I only go to the grocery if I need groceries, only go to the barber if I need a haircut, and only go to campgrounds when I need campground services. I also use campgrounds when we stay two or more nights in one location.

Like yours, my RV has those self-contained systems—so we use them. Being able to boondock provides you with thousands of new places to stay that must be avoided if you have convinced yourself that you must hook up to utilities for the night. Plus, since you paid all that extra money for the ability to boondock, you ought to try it occasionally.

Where to Boondock

When meandering across the US and Canada (as we commonly do), we regularly stay a night at Wal-Mart—but only with their permission. Other places you may be able to boondock overnight include Flying J (not the truck park but up front where

they allow RVs), Sam's Club, Cracker Barrel (only those that allow bus parking but their bus spaces can be pretty short), Fred Meyer stores, Giant food stores, Food Lion, Cabela's, Bass Pro Shops, Gander Mountain, Camping World, Rest Areas (along Interstates), some State Visitor Centers, some Lowe's, Home Depot, and malls, some organizations (Elks, Moose, VFW, American Legion), most casinos, some city parks, marinas, and others. With the exception of Rest Areas (along Interstates) and some State Visitor Centers, we **always ask permission** by calling ahead (if possible) or going in to ask if we could not call. Rest Areas and Visitor Centers typically have signs posted. Some, but not all, states allow you to just pull off the highway. Check before you do this and as always, be aware of your surroundings.

But Wal-Mart and those other businesses are not a campground so don't "camp" there—no grills, chairs, or awnings out. Don't even think of leaving your trash there! It's a convenient place to park overnight, period. So call ahead, ask permission, park, shop a bit, get/fix dinner, watch TV, sleep, and get up and leave. If you want to stay a few nights and be a tourist, get a campground.

> *A Personal Story...* We lost our brake lights on the motorhome and definitely did not want to drive at night. We had an appointment for service the next day. So we decided to pull into an Interstate Rest Area to stay the night. There were signs posted, "No Overnight Camping."
>
> I spotted a state trooper sitting in his car and walked over to ask if I could stay the night based on my safety issue. He said sure, they were providing 24-hour security in the Rest Area, would be there all night, and we were welcome to stay. I asked about the sign. He said that meant no tents. We had a noisy but good night.

I have recently heard estimates that there are approximately 500 municipalities across the USA that have banned overnight parking (city-wide). That number changes constantly based on local city councils voting in new ordinances or rescinding existing parking bans so it is best to call and verify. If overnight parking has been banned, don't go there and plan to park overnight. That's why you call ahead and ask. Interestingly, calling is the only way to get the current and correct information. Books, websites, and even your friend's previous experience may be out of date.

One suggestion for calling a municipality is to call the Chamber of Commerce (during business hours). If they do not know the actual ordinance, they can often suggest others for you to call and ask. Plus, they often suggest places within the city where you may park overnight. Additionally, I have also called the local police and county sheriff (on their non-emergency line) and asked where to stay.

An online group made up of RVers that own Discovery motorhomes use volunteers to maintain a large number of data files ready to upload into most common GPS software. You can find a lot of map-overlay files for your mapping software or stand-alone GPS. Most of their files are RV-related and compiled by fellow members of the Discovery Owner's Club. The files come with complete and easy instructions for adding those files to your GPS system. <**discoveryowners.com/cginfo.htm**>.

We **do not recommend** overnighting in the truck parks—those large parking areas next to truck stops. The major truck stop companies sometimes tolerate RVers parking on site but it's not encouraged. Indeed, many of the truckers don't like it either. They are required to get off the road (by law) and must have a place to park. Also, they are driving for a living so stay out of their way so they can do their jobs. Part of their job requirements is staying off the road (not driving) after so many hours. It doesn't matter if the truck park seems to have lots of room. All those truck spaces often fill up at some point and there is no way to judge just when it may happen.

Most Flying J's do allow RVs to park toward the front, out, away from the restaurant. Sometimes these areas will only accommodate two or three RVs so the spaces fill early. Other Flying J's have huge non-truck parking areas for their restaurant traffic and could easily accommodate numerous RVs without any congestion or problems.

Another reason for not staying in a truck park is the noise. Many truckers run their truck engines (idle) all night. Others may have unmuffled generators for their trailers. Either way, you should plan that it will be a loud night if you are parked next to a truck with its engine running.

The noise from the running truck engines are a fact of life when staying in a rest area, too. Plus, you have the noise of the trucks pulling in and departing all night. The engine noise along with the air brakes being applied and released is generally not equated to a pleasant night.

We have found that in some small towns, the local convenience store/gas station may have room for a couple of large rigs and often allow overnight parking—with permission, of course.

Rest Areas and Visitor Centers

Various states allow overnight parking in their Rest Areas and Visitor Centers. These are public areas, open to anyone to park for a while—enough to stretch your legs, maybe have a bite of lunch, or just use their restrooms. Not all of them allow overnight parking. If you use one, park in the designated truck-parking area if they do not have a specific RV parking area. I recommend parking your big motorhome with the trucks rather than the "trailer" area that some Rest Areas and Visitor Centers have. The trailer spaces are usually too short for a big rig towing a car.

According to the Alaskan State Trooper main information number, it is legal to pull off the highway and spend the night unless otherwise posted. The main criteria are that you must be at least 4-feet from the solid white line, must leave room for an additional vehicle, and of course, don't dump anything.

There are pull-offs and "official" rest areas everywhere — Alaska has more than I've seen anywhere else including Canada and the "Lower 48." I have seen as many as three per mile in some areas of the state and they were all nice and large! That's great for two reasons... First, it is illegal to block more than five vehicles driving behind you. Pull off and let them pass. The locals will appreciate it and some tourists (most likely RVers?) may be in a hurry. Second, you have a gazillion places to stay that are easy-access, clean, large, convenient, and free. Read more about this in *"RVing to Alaska."* <aboutrving.com>

The following information was available through the Texas website <traveltex.com> and is also great for RVers. Please note that all states and provinces will likely post similar information. This is presented here as a representative sampling only.

"Today more than a thousand Texas rest areas, picnic areas and scenic turnouts invite motorists to pause and relax from the concentration of driving. Often the site has been selected for its impressive landscape views, and each of the small parks is landscaped to complement its individual surroundings. All are equipped with shaded arbors, tables, benches and cooking grills. Remaining in a rest area for more than 24 hours or erecting any kind of structure is prohibited by law." (2007 Texas Travel Guide)

This does not imply that every pull-off or rest area is secure. As we have stated previously, you must use lots of common sense when pulling off for the night. Personally, we would rather be in a somewhat busier Rest Area than a lonely  one—and we have been in both—and we haven't had a single problem. Again, it just makes sense to put up with a bit more noise while feeling a bit more secure.

If there is a question as to whether you can park overnight at a particular rest area, use the Motor Carrier's Atlas mentioned earlier to find the toll-free number and make a non-emergency call to the state police and ask. You will need the highway number and mile-marker (or some description of the location you are questioning) when you call.

Enough is Enough

My Focus

It was my goal to find and furnish you with enough current information, facts, data, and in some cases, speculation about what to do to help you initially discuss, plan for, and start fulltiming or at least get ready to take that extended trip. I talked with a large number of people—some were RVers and some weren't. I was amazed at how many non-RVers said they had thought about "just taking off in an RV" but simply blew off the idea as silly, impractical, or ridiculous. While my sympathy goes out to them, it's not a lifestyle for everyone. If it was, it would be more crowded!

As I said at the beginning of the book, this is…

"Not about trying to talk you into fulltiming. I would never attempt to talk you into this. You have to either want to or at least be intrigued enough by the idea that you are willing to try it."

But for those of you that do try it, you have my best wishes and a sincere "Good Luck" in your efforts. Remember, I'm here to help and I know a lot of resources where you can get help. So, if you have a question, comment, complaint, or just want to say hello, here's my e-mail address. Don't hesitate to send me a note at…

fulltime@aboutrving.com

Thanks for reading this far.

I hope this collection of information helps.

Let me know if it does.

R. E. Jones

–Notes–

–Notes–

–Notes–

Looking for a Seminar?
E-mail me!

Contact the author direct at…

fulltime@aboutrving.com

Looking for a Great Gift?
Give the Book!
Tell your Friends, too!

Order Online

aboutrving.com

Contact the author direct at…

fulltime@aboutrving.com

Try these...

They make Great Gifts!
aboutrving.com